Workbook for Caretakers
of
End-Stage Alcoholics

Linda Bartee Doyne

(aka LindaJane Riley)

The Immortal Alcoholic's Wife

DEDICATION

This book is dedicated to all my blog readers and anyone who has the task of care taking an alcoholic. No matter what stage the alcoholic is in, eventually you will need this book.

TABLE of CONTENTS

WELCOME TO THE WORKBOOK

for

Caretakers of End-Stage Alcoholics

The life of a caretaker is not a walk in the park and sometimes people take on the task without understanding what to expect. There are three sections concerning some of the basic physical characteristics of end-stage alcoholism and the associated cleanliness issues. It's an extremely stressful lifestyle and maintaining some aspect of peace and sanity is a gigantic issue. You will find a section on suggestions for the caretakers maintenance of their own sanity.

Within these pages you will find a means of tracking the health and history of the end-stage alcoholic in your care. When entering a medical facility you will be asked questions that may be difficult to answer because you simply did not notice or just do not know. If you get into the habit of tracking certain information you will be able to give a good account of what happened and when. This may be vital information in determining the level of need for medical intervention.

Before you go to the hospital, make a copy of the information in this book and take it with you. Have the med tech add these pages to the chart to provide a complete history. Point out to the physician that you have provided these pages. Physically show him the pages you have submitted. Don't just tell him/her – show them the actual pages. By doing this, the information becomes a part of that hospital's permanent medical record as well as providing valuable immediate information.

It's also important to know how to communicate with the medical community. Besides explaining how to use this workbook, there is a suggested method of talking with the medical staff. Read it, learn it, and use it, in order to establish good co-operative communications with your doctor.

Medical directives are important pieces of paper to have within your grasp in a moments notice. This workbook provides explanations of the various types of legal documents and a place for them to be easily accessible. Because alcoholics can be very resistant to signing these documents, there is an outline of a suggested format for getting what you want.

Before filling out the forms or inserting information, read (at least glance) the entire workbook in order to get familiar with the contents. Then use it as a tool to help you in your journey through the impossible and frustrating world of end-stage alcoholism

DISCLAIMER

The following is a list of things that I do NOT claim to be:

- A medical professional in any capacity;

- A counselor or social worker of any sort;

- A legal professional at any level;

- A representative of any rehabilitation center;

- An employee of any pharmaceutical endeavor;

- A member of any anti-alcohol organization;

- An affiliate of any governmental agency.

The following is a list of all the things that I DO claim to be:

- The wife of an end-stage alcoholic;

- The mother of a child who died as a result of alcoholism;

- The step-parent of a son whose entire family died after being hit by a drunk-driver;

- A member of a family that has had many drug issues;

- An advocate of safe driving and healthy living through responsible choices;

- Founder of OARS Support Groups for family and friends of alcoholics;

- The author of The Immortal Alcohol blog (www.immortalalcoholic.blogspot.com);

- Author of *The Immortal Alcoholics Wife* and *That Reminds Me;*

- Contributor to HBO's upcoming documentary, *Risky Drinking.*

This workbook is a result of my experiences, research and drive to simplify the life of anyone who finds themselves as a caretaker of an end-stage alcoholic. To learn more about me, please read my blog. –

Linda Bartee Doyne

MY SIMPLIFIED STORY

I am a 60+ year old woman who spent more than 20 years in the center of my alcoholic husband's insanity. We separated after our two children had grown. There was no divorce because I didn't want to jeopardize losing my military benefits after contributing so many years to his military career. I also knew that eventually one of my children would step in to try to take care of him as my husband became more ill. I didn't want that to happen.

In 2009 my husband, Riley, was living with two terrific roommates. One was a circuit court judge who was thriving in spite of having muscular dystrophy. The other roommate was a nurse/caretaker for the judge.

We had just lost our son to alcohol abuse and my daughter and I were devastated. We needed the support we provided for each other and knew that it was imperative for me to make the 3,000 mile move from California to North Carolina. At that point, I had no intention to move Riley with me.

When Riley's roommates called and told they were going to have him committed as being a danger to himself and others, I thought – good. But, then I found out that my daughter was making plans to bring him to North Carolina and take care of him.

There was no way I would allow my daughter's life to be consumed by the affects of her father's alcoholism. I moved him back into my home and he has been here ever since.

For more on my story and journey please go to my blog site www.immortalalcoholic.blogspot.com or read *The Immortal Alcoholic's Wife*.

•

How to Use the Workbook

This workbook was created to help the caretaker know and understand exactly where the alcoholic stands in terms of the alcoholic's physical health. It can bridge the communication gap between the caretaker and the medical professional. Used properly you may end up with answers to questions that you don't want to ask out loud.

1) You will find lots of blank pages in this book for your notes and thoughts

2) Read this workbook through to get an understanding of what information will be used.

3) Buy a three ring binder and divider pages

4) Label the dividers as follows:

    a) Basic Information

    b) Current / On-Going Complications

    c) Resolved Illnesses

    d) Family History

    e) Vital Signs and Current Conditions

    f) General Lab Work

    g) MELD Score

    h) Child-Pugh Score

    i) Detox History

    j) Rehab History

    k) Websites / References

    l) Notes / Journal or place in the back binder cover pocket.

    m) Medical Directive / POA

5) Copy the pages from this book and separate them into the appropriate binder section.

6) On the binder's left side front cover pocket, place all the pages that are shown in the Overall Condition section.

7) Fill in all information that you have available to you.

8) Update the pages as you receive lab reports and other observations.

Using Information from Your Workbook

If you are seeing a doctor for the first time, take a copy of all the pages containing information, such as, Medical History, Family History, Current Complications, and all the legal stuff.

Make sure you request that the info be added to your alcoholic's medical chart. But hold on to the Overall Condition pages until you are actually in the room with the doctor.

When the doctor asks the reason for your visit, let your alcoholic give his side of the story. Expect him/her to lie but don't correct or interrupt while he/she is talking. When the alcoholic is done, speak up and tell the doctor you have recorded his condition as you have observed and hand him your graph. Explain what the graph represents – the alcoholic's condition on a scale of 1 to 28 based on 1 as being in excellent condition and 28 as the worst.

The reason for your visit is that you suspect that he may have "Hepatitic Encephalopathy" and/or "Cirrhosis" and **you would like his opinion**. It's very important to ask for exactly what you want and tell exactly what you suspect. Use proper medical terminology. If the doctor may appear to brush you off – don't walk out the door yet. The goal is to get an order for blood work that will supply you with information needed to determine his true status. Be polite. Be respectful. You can be mad as hell later – but for now – be the epitome of the concerned caretaker seeking help from someone more knowledgeable than you.

If you don't like the doctor or he/she doesn't help you get what you need – find another doctor and try again.

If you don't hear back from the doctor within a week with lab results, call them and ask when to expect the report to be available. Keep calling. When the results are in, tell the doctor's office you will pick up a copy of the report or have them mail it to you.

When you have the report in your hands, transfer the information into the proper places in on your workbook pages.

Continue this process and you will develop your own cache of valuable information concerning the health of your alcoholic.

.

A Bit About the Medical Community

Before reading the rest of this, keep this in mind: **The goal is to get LAB WORK and/or an AIDE and/or HOSPICE** (when the time comes).

It takes a long time, a lot of money, and an excruciating amount of hard work to become a medical professional. People don't go into this profession just because they have nothing better to do. To be an addictionologist, they must take other specific courses and workshops following the many years of formal education, internship, residency, etc. The addiction world is ever changing – there a new drug invented every day and they must stay up to date.

For the most part, you will not be taking your alcoholic to a doctor who specializes in addiction medicine because those doctors are usually found in rehab centers. Instead you'll be seeing a doctor or medical professional who has one goal and that is to save lives. For them, to be confronted with an alcoholic, who clearly doesn't want to have a viable, productive life, must be very frustrating for them. Why should they care what condition the alcoholic is in if they cannot persuade them to want to live? It must feel like a gigantic waste of their time. After all, the majority of their patients want to live – they have cancer patients who cling to hope for a continued life. That's the nature of the business they are in and it is their job to try to get the alcoholic into rehab and help them recover to a healthy life.

As caretakers, we expect a lot from the medical community. In some cases, we expect them to just accept that the alcoholic is dying and for them to help us monitor their decline. But, that is contrary to what the doctors must do which is to try to save the alcoholic's life – or at least lengthen it. If it's a new doctor to you, they haven't taken the same journey as you with this alcoholic– they aren't ready to give up.

The workbook will help you explain how you've come to the conclusions that you have and will document those conclusions. It helps the doctor see your side. His side is to offer detox or rehab. It never hurts to offer. Who knows – the alcoholic might agree and recover. That would be good. Most likely the alcoholic will NOT agree and the doctor may turn to the caretaker and provide assistance in monitoring the condition. That is truly what we want as caretakers – assistance.

If you can put yourself in the shoes of the medical person, you will find it easier to communicate how you would like the doctor to help you take care of the alcoholic. It will not serve the caretaker well to take an "I know more than you" attitude. Instead, admit that you may not have all the answers and ask for help.

A typical scenario that I've been confronted with has the doctor enter the room and introduce himself. Then he asks how he can help you today or what has brought you to his office. Let the alcoholic say that he doesn't know why he's there or whatever it is he's going to say. The doctor by this time is listening to the lungs or has begun some kind of examination. Let the doctor do his thing. Let the alcoholic say his piece.

At this point the doctor will say something like – he's not sure what he can do or he'll suggest getting some blood work. Wait for a break in the conversation. Be patient and when there is a moment of silence after all the above has taken place – it will be your time to speak.

Tell the doctor that the alcoholic is drinking however much he is drinking and that you have observed a marked decline in his condition. Show him the graph and explain as outlined in Number 3 of "How to take advantage of this workbook." Tell the doctor that you're concerned that he may have one of the many alcohol related complications and tell him why you think that. You can use the Vital Statistics pages from the workbook.

Use the correct medical terminology for whatever the complication is that you want addressed. Instead of stating a fact – "He has gastritis" -- put it in the form of a suspicion – "I think he may have gastritis." You are not the professional. You are not qualified to make a diagnosis. Let the doctor make the diagnosis. That's his job. The important thing is that you now have the doctor's attention. He now sees you as an aid to doing his job instead of someone that must be dealt with or placated.

It is OK for you to request a blood test to find out how his liver is functioning or how much ammonia is in his system. The key word here is REQUEST. A demand for anything will only get you hostility and negativity. Try using this **"Would it be possible to get a complete blood test that covers most everything?"**

Don't take up a lot of the doctor's time telling him exactly about the outrageous thing that the alcoholic did last night. Of course, if he asks for specific examples of the outrageous activities then give him specifics.

If a doctor makes you angry or treats you with hostility, it will do you no good to enter into an argument. I once had a doctor tell me that there was nothing wrong with my husband and that we didn't need a medical doctor, but rather a counselor. I was livid. I left there in a hurry – but I left without a request for lab work. My pride and "know-it-all-ness" caused me to fail to reach my goal of getting a lab report and eventually -- hospice. Three weeks later, my husband was admitted to the hospital after having a stroke.

Some doctors simply won't see alcoholics. Go through the phone book. Call the doctor's office and ask the nurse if the doctor has very much experience with treating alcoholic patients. That might keep you away from hostile medical providers.

Once you've found a good doctor that you can work with as a team – treat him/her like gold. They are rare.

If you don't have insurance

Many alcoholics have no insurance and/or refuse to go to the doctor. In that case, try to get the alcoholic to agree to lab work. You don't need a doctor's order to get lab work if you are willing to pay for it out of your own pocket. Call the labs in your area and ask if they do that and how much they charge. This may be the only way to get the lab report if you have a stubborn alcoholic who refuses medical treatment. Sometimes labs will come to you home to collect the sample.

Just a warning – some tests can be as much as $400. So if you have insurance, do your best to go through the doctor.

WHAT TO EXPECT

The best thing you can expect from an alcoholic is NOTHING. The end-stage alcoholic usually has nothing to offer in the category of co-operation, support, assistance or respect. As the alcoholism progresses, the body and mind deteriorates. The following will begin to be daily occurrences:

1   Loss of interest in family;

2   Loss of short-term memory;

3   Reversed sleeping cycle – with waking hours steadily decreasing;

4   Inability for blood to clot – excessive nosebleeds;

5   Vomiting;

6   Falls easily and has difficulty getting up;

7   No muscle strength;

8   Loss of bladder and bowel control;

9   Inappropriate social behavior – loss of moral values;

10   Easily agitated with possible increasing violent tendencies;

11   Personal hygiene disappears;

12   Loss of appetite for food -- sporadic eating habits.

THE CARETAKERS CHORES

When the alcoholism reaches end-stage it is impossible for the alcoholic to tend to his own cleanliness of self or his environment. The end-stage alcoholic seldom showers or bathes, brushes their teeth, shampoos their hair, or washes their hands. Because they often have feces or urine on their hands, clothing, bedding, and/or anywhere in their living space or bathroom facilities, it becomes imperative that the caretaker take precautions to prevent others from coming in contact the soiled areas and items.

Illnesses that can be transferred to healthy household members include Salmonella, E.coli, Hepatitis, Giardiasis, Dysentery, worms and other viral and bacterial illnesses. All of these illnesses are extremely serious, highly contagious, and can even be deadly. Contracting these illnesses is not just by means of touching the feces, but it can also enter though breathing in minor particles or through cracks on calloused feet.

After having been diagnosed with Salmonella, I asked the doctor why, if Riley were carrying these illnesses, wasn't he sick? His explanation was that Riley's system has grown immune to the affects of the illnesses. He has the illness, but does not get sick from it. It's also the reason why Riley can eat spoiled food and never get sick. On the other hand, the end-stage alcoholic vomits often anyway, so it may be difficult to determine the exact cause other than the drinking.

If others are to live in the same household with an end-stage alcoholic, certain chores must be done on a regular basis. This is the only way to less the probability of a spread of the contamination.

Always **wear latex gloves, a surgical mask, hospital gown or apron , and solid soled shoes with surgical booties** when doing the chores listed below. Also use a cleaning solution of 1 part bleach to 2 parts hot water which will neutralize most bacteria.

1 -- Clean the toilet, lower walls, floors and sink of the primary bathroom used by the alcoholic. I do this once a month, but it would be better for it to be done more often.

2 -- Use waterproof pads on the chairs most often used by the alcoholic. This will save you from having to throw out furniture cushions or furniture. I change these when they appear to be soiled, but at least once a week.

3 -- Put waterproof pads between the mattress and the bottom sheet on the alcoholic's bed. You can buy waterproof sheets, but I also use the disposable pads so I can just throw them away.

4 -- Change the sheets every other day.

5 -- Change the blankets at least one a month or if they appear soiled. I use the simple cotton blankets like the ones at the hospital so that I can easily wash them in bleachy water.

6 -- Do the alcoholic's laundry separate from the family wash. Cross contamination can occur even in the process of washing the clothing and bedding. I do all Riley's laundry and then run an empty load in a quick cycle with hot water and bleach which washes out the tub of the washer.

7 -- Lay out clean clothes for the alcoholic every day. The alcoholic probably won't put them on, but at least you tried.

8 -- If you can -- get him to take a shower daily in a tub/shower equipped with a seat and grab bars. I have been unsuccessful at this. Most end-stage alcoholics have no interest in personal hygiene. They seem to oblivious to the fact that they smell like a walking sewer system.

9 -- Make every attempt to keep him from handling family food. Since the alcoholic isn't concerned with hand-washing, he will contaminate the family food if he handles it.

10 -- Take him to a salon for hair cutting, shampooing, manicures and pedicures. I make sure that Riley washes his hands before we leave for the salon. I also take with me a pair of latex gloves for the stylist to use when washing his hair. Once his hair is washed, feet in the soak and hands washed, it is safe to cut, pedi and mani.

Once you have finished all the cleaning chores, it is time to remove the protective coverings.

1 -- First remove the shoe booties

2 -- Remove the gown

3 -- Remove the latex gloves

4 -- Wash your hands with anti-bacterial soap

5 -- Remove the surgical mask

I know all this sounds like over-kill, but it is worth it to prevent being locked in your room away from the family because you are contagious – or spending hours sitting on the toilet because your bowels are doing a war dance. Salmonella is no fun.

TIPS FOR MAINTAINING SANITY

The caretaker must take special care to prevent burn-out and health issues related to stress. Unfortunately, the caretaker often will display symptoms of stress-related disorders long before the alcoholic reaches the end. As a caretaker, I live by a certain set of standards that helps me keep things in perspective and give me a better life. I've listed them here.

1 -- Be a rational realist. You did not cause the alcoholism. You cannot cure it. There are only two ways out – sobriety or death. In the case of end-stage alcoholism, this is a terminal illness.

2 -- Take care of your physical health. Stress of caretaking an alcoholic can lead to health issues for the caretaker. It is not uncommon for the caretaker to have heart issues, hypertension, and stroke, and/or develop asthma and/or insomnia. Go to your medical doctor regularly for check-ups, flu shots, etc.

3 -- Take care of your mental health. Find a therapist that has experience with caretakers of alcoholics. This can help you keep your perspective.

4 -- Keep your objectivity. It's not your illness. The end-stage alcoholic is no longer the person you fell in love with or took care of you as a child. That person is gone and has been replaced by the pod people leaving you with a person you don't recognize. Grieve the loss, feel the hurt – when you do that the worst is over.

5 -- Maintain your own life. End-stage alcoholics take a lot of time away from everyone else in the household because they have to be monitored for everyone's protection. That doesn't mean the caretaker should stop doing the things they love. Find a person who can stay with the alcoholic while you do whatever it is you want to do. If the alcoholic can still be left at home alone – take advantage of it. Focus on your passion -- quilting, scrapbook, cooking, painting, writing, woodworking, being musical. Let your passion be your escape.

6 -- Establish a support network. These systems are everywhere. Besides the standard Al-Anon (which doesn't always fit for the end-stage caretaker), there are forums on sites such as about.alcoholism.com or soberrecovery.com, blogs written by people who have been caretakers, personal friends and family. Develop and nurture these relationships because they will give you someone to vent to, other than your therapist.

7 -- Educate yourself about alcoholism. Knowledge is the key to survival. The more you know the more you will find surviving easier. Search the web, ask questions from others. Do your homework. It won't save the alcoholic, but it will fill up that space in your brain that is always whispering – what if…

8 -- Find enjoyable distractions. When the alcoholic is just raging about this or that, or if he's spilled his drink for the 50th time today, take a mental break. I love the old commercial that goes – Calgon, take me away! So I fill up the tub with lots of bubbles and spend a little time in some imaginary place far away. Sometimes I only get 15 minutes – but its 15 minutes that can restore my sanity.

9 -- Find the comedy. It's everywhere. Even the most serious of events can have a humorous side. Alcoholism is an absurd condition associated with outlandish actions. Have ever said – if it wasn't so sad, it would be funny? Well take out the "sad" and just make it funny. Laugh. Laugh as often as you can and for as long as you can. You will feel better for it.

10 -- Be sure to enjoy every sunrise and sunset.

GENERAL HEALTH INFORMATION

NAME OF ALCOHOLIC				
CURRENT AGE			BIRTHDATE	
DAILY CONSUMPTION (Liters - LT / Ounces - OZ)			DRINK OF CHOICE	
LAST DAY OF SOBRIETY			AGE AT FIRST DRINK	
NUMBER OF TIMES IN DETOX		NUMBER OF TIMES IN REHAB		
LAST DETOX FACILITY NAME				
Date of Admittance		Phone Number		
Address				
Notes				
LAST REHAB CENTER NAME				
Date of Admittance		Phone Number		
Address				
Notes				
CARETAKERS NAME, Relationship				
EMERGENCY CONTACT NAME, Relationship				
Emergency Contact Phone Number		Other / Cell		
SECONDARY CONTACT NAME, Relationship				
Secondary Phone Number		Other / Cell		
INTERNIST / PHYSICIAN NAME				
Internist / Physician Contact Info				
THERAPIST/COUNSELOR NAME				
Therapist/Counselor Contact Info				
OTHER CONTACT INFO				
Contact Phone Number		Other / Cell		
OTHER ILLNESS / CONDITIONS				
Date of Onset				
Prognosis				
OTHER ILLNESS / CONDITION				
Date of Onset				
Prognosis				
PRIMARY MEDICAL INSURANCE				
Policy Number / Group Number Information				
SECONDARY MEDICAL INSURANCE				
Policy Number / Group Number Information				

Medical History

On the next page you will find a chart for indicating any diagnosis of previous conditions that the patient may have been treated in the past.

NOTE: All forms are included at the end of the book where it can be removed and photocopied allowing it to be inserted into a binder.

Condition	Current	Resolved
Anemia		
Arthritis		
Asthma / Allergies		
Bleeding Problems		
Cancer		
Cirrhosis		
Delirium Tremens		
Dementia		
Diabetes		
Epilepsy		
Esophageal Bleeding		
Gastritis / Ulcers		
Glaucoma		
Heart Disease / Issues		
Hepatic Encephalopathy		
Hepatitis		
High Cholesterol		
Hypertension / High Blood Pressure		
Kidney Diseases		
Migraine Headaches		
Oriental Flushing Syndrome		
Osteoarthritis		
Osteoporosis		
Pancreatitis		
Polyneuropathy / Neurological Issues		
Rheumatoid Arthritis		
Stroke		
Thyroid Disorders		
Vision Issues		
Wernicke-Korsakoff		
OTHER:		

Current / On-Going Conditions

Condition	Date diagnosed	Date Lasted treated	Notes / Prognosis

Resolved Conditions

Condition	Date diagnosed	Date Lasted treated	Notes / Prognosis

Family History

Relative	Living	Health Issues	Deceased (mo/yr)	Cause of death
Father				
Mother				
Sibling (M or F)				
Sibling (M or F)				
Sibling (M or F)				
Sibling (M or F)				
Child (M or F)				
Child (M or F)				
Child (M or F)				
Child (M or F)				
Child (M or F)				

Conditions	Father	Mother	Sibling	Child	NOTES
Alcoholism					
Alzheimer's Disease					
Arthritis					
Asthma / Allergies					
Cancer					
Dementia					
Diabetes					
Epilepsy					
Gastritis / Ulcers					
Glaucoma					
Heart Disease / Issues					
Hepatitis					
High Cholesterol					
Hypertension / High Blood Pressure					
Kidney Diseases					
Lupus					
Migraine Headaches					
Osteoporosis					
Pancreatitis					
Polyneuropathy / Neurological Issues					
Stroke					
Thyroid Disorders					
OTHER:					

ALCOHOL AND BIOLOGY

To understand how alcohol damages the biological functioning of the human body, you must understand how the body processes the alcohol.

Once an alcoholic drink has passed our lips it travels down through the esophagus to the stomach where it is absorbed into the bloodstream. Once in the bloodstream, alcohol goes to every part of the body.

To get rid of the alcohol, it is eliminated through the metabolic system. Metabolism of alcohol takes place in the liver. The liver detoxifies the alcohol and removes it from the bloodstream. This prevents the alcohol from accumulating and destroying cells and organs. Some portions of the alcohol are excreted through the breath and sweat glands. In some cases not all the alcohol is metabolized in the first pass through the liver and will continue through the bloodstream until it can be metabolized completely.

The alcohol that has been metabolized in the liver creates metabolic waste which is filtered once again by the kidneys while controlling the bodily fluid balance. The more liquid a person consumes the harder the kidneys have to work to eliminate the fluid.

The kidneys send the fluid to the bladder and then it is sent on its journey into the sewer system.

Sounds pretty simple.

The system gets complicated when the liver cannot metabolize all the alcohol thus sending it back through the bloodstream over and over again. The toxins (which in fact are poisons), one of which is plasma ammonia, accumulate in various organs. All this build-up of toxins leads to one or more of the following conditions.

28

Cirrhosis

Because this is the best known alcohol related disease, I decided this would be the best place to start my research.

With the consumption of large quantities of alcohol, the liver becomes scarred and the scar tissue blocks the flow of blood through the portal vein. The portal vein carries blood from the intestines to the liver. The more scar tissue created the less the blood the liver can process. The liver is a "blood cleaner" tool. If the liver doesn't function properly, the affect will be more toxins, such as plasma ammonia, not being eliminated. The blood will begin to thin and contain more toxins which in turn creates the increased risk of infection.

Some of the signs and symptoms of a malfunctioning liver include:

- Jaundice -- yellowing of the skin and eyes

- Fatigue and weakness

- Loss of appetite, nausea

- Red spider-like blood vessels visible just under the skin

- Swelling of extremities, such as hands, legs, feet from fluid build-up

- Swelling of the belly

As the liver damage increases other diseases develop. The liver is a miraculous organ because it can regenerate some potions of itself if the alcoholic ceases ingesting alcohol permanently. However, the scarring will remain and each time alcohol consumption resumes the less time is required for additional scarring to begin. By the time cirrhosis has been diagnosed, other complications have usually developed that are not as forgiving as the liver.

Alcoholic Pancreatitis

The pancreas is a small organ with three purposes: 1) provide digestive enzymes; 2) provide insulin and glucagon hormones; and, 3) secrete large amounts of sodium bicarbonate. The three functions all aid in the digestion of food, regulating sugar levels and neutralize acid in the stomach.

Pancreatitis is an inflammation of the pancreas. The metabolism of the alcohol in the pancreas is similar to the function of the liver. The metabolic process creates by-products when, in excessive amounts, accumulate in the ducts and create a blockage. If the blockage continues, the enzymes begin to digest the cells of the pancreas. The pancreas becomes inflamed and ceases to function.

Symptoms of alcohol induced pancreatitis can include:

- Yellowing of the eyes
- Back pain
- Nausea and vomiting
- Fever
- Diarrhea
- Lack of appetite

Hepatic Encephalopathy

With the liver not functioning properly, the plasma ammonia levels raise and are transported to the brain via the bloodstream. The ammonia makes a home in the frontal lobe of the brain and interferes with brain's function.

Some symptoms of hepatic encephalopathy may include:

- Lack of awareness (Is not aware of actions taking place around him)
- Inverted sleep pattern (Sleeping all day and staying awake all night)
- Irritability (Everything is a source of irritation – mostly imagined)
- Tremors (Uncontrollable trembling or shaking movements)
- Somnolence (A strong desire for sleep or sleeping for prolonged periods of time)
- Asterixis (Uncontrollable movements of the arms and wrists)
- Ascites (Accumulation of fluid in the peritoneal cavity)
- Disorientation (Confusion as to place, time, people)
- Amnesia (Inability to remember day to day or even longer)
- Uninhibited behavior (Ignoring personal hygiene, use of foul language in the presence of children, anything society would deem inappropriate)
- Seizures, Coma and Death (eventually, if untreated)

Whether or not the damage is permanent depends on how long the alcoholic has been abusing. Some of the symptoms will disappear during the detox process, but some may never go away. The ability to remember is sometimes greatly hampered even when sobriety has been attained, leaving the alcoholic with dementia.

This disease is graded as to the severity based on the West Haven Criteria.

Grade 1 –   Trivial lack of awarene

   Shortened attention span

   Euphoria or anxiety

Grade 2 –   Lethargy or apathy

   Minimal disorientation

   Subtle personality change

   Inappropriate behavior

Grade 3 –   Somnolence to semi-stupor, responsive to verbal stimuli

Confusion

Gross disorientation, bizarre   behavior

Grade 4 –   Coma (unresponsive to verbal stimuli)

I guess there is no grade for DEAD.

Hepatic Encephalopathy leads to or is somehow connect to Wernicke-Korsakoff Syndrome.

Wernicke-Korsakoff Syndrome

This is a condition resulting from a thiamine (Vitamin B1) deficiency. When alcoholics stop eating balanced meals, they lose valuable vitamins and minerals necessary for the body to function properly.

The symptoms may include:

- Confusion;

- Tremors;

- Changes in vision;

- Loss of short-term and long-term memories;

- Hallucinations;

- Muscle weakness and atrophy;

- Lack of coordination;

- Appearance of poor nutrition.

Delirium Tremens

Latin for "shaking frenzy", Delirium Tremens (DTs) are also known as "the shakes". DTs occur upon the cessation of alcohol consumption after a long period of habitual drinking in large quantities. The condition carries a 5% mortality rate with treatment and 35% without treatment.

Symptoms usually don't occur until between the second and tenth day of alcohol withdrawal. They include:

- Tremors of the extremities
- Confusion
- Diarrhea
- Insomnia
- Disorientation
- Agitation
- Hallucinations
- Anxiety
- High pulse, blood pressure and breathing rate

Treatment includes the use of medication such as benzodiazepines, such as Valium, Ativan or Librium. Additional drugs are used to control the hallucinations.

It is never advisable for an alcoholic to go it "cold turkey" without any medical assistance. It may seem brave, but bravery is often met with death.

Esophageal Varices

An esophageal varices occurs when the scarring on the liver prevents blood from flowing through the liver sending that blood flow through the veins in the esophagus. The lining of the esophagus is irritated by the alcohol as it travels down the throat and into the stomach. The alcohol is caustic and wears away the mucus membrane. The blood vessels become thin and the walls weaken. The pressure from the extra blood flow causes the esophagus to balloon outward and rupture. When the rupture occurs, the bleeding may be extremely rapid and death can be imminent.

There are no warning symptoms for this condition unless there is a bleeding "drip" rather than a rupture. That is, the bleeding may be only a small tear in the esophagus. In this case there may be symptoms of:

- Black, tarry, "coffee-ground", and/or bloody stools;

- Light-headedness;

- Paleness;

- Vomiting and/or vomiting of blood

Since alcohol is a blood thinning agent, any tiny tear or lesion can become a life-threatening situation. Alcoholics have been known to bleed into the stomach and the alcoholic eventually bleeds to death before anyone would notice.

Ascites

Ever notice that your alcoholic's tummy is starting to look like a "baby bump"? It could be the start of ascites which is a swelling in the stomach area due to an accumulation of fluid in the peritoneal cavity. It can also manifest with swelling in the ankles and legs (peripheral oedema). There are three classifications or grades:

Grade 1 =   Mild, only visible on ultrasound and CT

Grade 2 =   Detectable with flank bulging

Grade 3 =   Directly visible

LIVER TRANSPLANT

Riley once told me he had a plan. The plan was to drink for as long as he could – until he was near death. Then he would detox, stop drinking for six months and apply to UNOS for a new liver. After the transplant he would resume his trip down Alcoholism Lane. I think he's in for a rude awakening because I discovered that only 14% of all transplantable livers go to alcoholics.

Approximately 95% of alcoholics with cirrhosis **never** receive referrals for a transplant because they cannot stop drinking long enough to even begin the process of meeting the requirements. UNOS (United Network of Organ Sharing) has strict guidelines for alcoholics needing a new liver as a result of cirrhosis. They must:

- Abstain from alcohol consumption for a minimum of six
- months;
- Completion of a substance abuse program;
- Weekly attendance at Alcoholics Anonymous meetings;
- Successfully passing a psychological examination;
- Regular comprehensive physical examinations.

Once on the list, if any of the requirements are not met or if the alcoholic slips, they are permanently removed from the list

People are prioritized and placed on a transplant list using a formula to determine life expectancy without a new liver. The ones with the shortest time left to live were closer to the top.

There were two formulas – the MELD Score and Child-Pugh Score. I found information on Wikipedia.

What is a MELD Score?

If a person with a failing liver is fortunate enough to manage to get on the UNOS list for transplantation, the person is evaluated for the chance of survival without the transplant.

Typically the determination is made by assigning a MELD (Model for End-Stage Liver Disease) Score which is a number calculated by using information obtained from three segments of a blood test. The resulting score will determine the severity of the disease and predicts the chance of survival over the next three months. Liver transplant patients are placed on the waiting list based on who has the shortest life expectancy without the transplant. The MELD Score is used, along with other factors, in making that determination.

When the doctor orders a blood test, he will include in the order a Comprehensive Metabolic Panel along with Prothrombin Time (PT) with whatever else he is ordering. These tests will provide the information you need for determining the MELD Score.

Please see the section in Lab Reports for determining MELD Score.

What is the CHILD-PUGH Score?

This score is also used in determining the possible life expectancy of a person with liver disease. However, it uses two additional factors and estimates the prognosis of survival for one or two years. Points are given for each measurement, the points are then added up to get the prognosis result. The two additional factors are **ASCITES** and **HEPATIC ENCEPHALOPATHY.**

Please see the section in Lab Reports for determining Child-Pugh Score.

VITAL SIGNS / CURRENT CONDITION

This is the type of information a visiting nurse would record. If possible, complete the following form with the patient's information on at least a weekly basis. Make copies of the blank chart page and add it to your workbook for additional space.

Record the date, temperature, pulse, blood pressure (bystolic/dystolic) and respiratory rate. Use the below chart to determine the level of urinary continence, bowel control, stool consistency, functional status, skin color and eye clarity. Enter the level number in the daily chart. Use the lower point level the issue is not almost but not quite the full Level. Add the points for all the items in the green area and add to those numbers to the chart at the end of this workbook which will track the alcoholic's overall condition.

Issue	Level 1 – No Points	Level 2 – 1-2 Point	Level 3 – 2-3 points
Urinary Continence	No incontinence	Some incontinence	No bladder control
Bowel Control	No lack of control	Some lack of control	No bowel control
Stool Consistency	Normal	Diarrhea	Coffee ground consistency
Mobility Status	Walks without aid	Falls occasionally	Cannot walk without assistance
Food Intake Level	3 meals daily – no vomiting	2 meals – some vomiting	Less than 2 meals – most often with vomiting
Hygiene Level	Showers 1x weekly	Showers 1x monthly	Does not shower
Skin Color	Rosecea (red, no yellow)	Rosecea (redness on checks and nose) Yellowing around eyes	Back and/or stomach area yellow/green
Eye Clarity	Clear	Yellow whites	Yellow/golden film over entire eye covering pupils
Urinary Continence	No incontinence	Some incontinence	No bladder control
Bowel Control	No lack of control	Some lack of control	No bowel control
Stool Consistency	Normal	Diarrhea	Coffee ground consistency
Mobility Status	Walks without aid	Falls occasionally	Cannot walk without assistance
Food Intake Level	3 meals daily – no vomiting	2 meals – some vomiting	Less than 2 meals – most often with vomiting
Hygiene Level	Showers 1x weekly	Showers 1x monthly	Does not shower
Skin Color	Rosecea (red, no yellow)	Rosecea (redness on checks and nose) Yellowing around eyes	Back and/or stomach area yellow/green
Eye Clarity	Clear	Yellow whites	Yellow/golden film over entire eye covering pupils

49

Vital Sign / Current Condition Chart

		Time	
Temperature		Pulse	
Blood Pressure		Respiratory Rate	
Urinary Continence		Bowel Control	
Stool Consistency		Mobility Status	
Food Intake		Hygiene Level	
Skin Color		Eye Clarity	
TOTAL POINTS			

LAB RESULTS

Request a copy of all lab reports ordered by the doctor. Put the reports in this section of the workbook. Using the information on the reports and your own observations, you can determine the status of the alcoholic's liver functioning and the build up of toxins in the brain, as well as determine the MELD (Model for End-Stage Liver Disease) or the Child-Pugh Score.

Sample Lab Report

Review the Sample Lab Report (**Page 46**) to give you an idea of what to look for on your alcoholic's report.

General Blood Test Results

INR – This relates to the time it takes for the blood to coagulate. Normal range is 0.8-1.2. The higher the result, the longer it takes for the blood to clot which means that the blood is thinner than normal.

PROTHROMBIN TIME – This also refers to the time it takes for the blood to coagulate. Normal range is 8.7-11.5. Again, the higher the result, the longer it takes for the blood to clot which means the blood is thinner than normal.

AMMONIA, PLASM – This relates to the amount of ammonia (toxins) in his blood and are not being flushed out of his body. The higher the build up of toxins, the higher the score and the more likely the alcoholic has Hepatic Encephalopathy. Normal range is 27-102.

MAGNESIUM, SERUM – Used to determine the amount of magnesium in the body. Magnesium is necessary for muscles and nerves to function normally. It also aids in controlling blood sugar levels, immune system, heart beat and blood pressure. The lower the score on the lab report, the more likely there will be issues in these areas. Normal range is 1.6-2.6.

RBC – Red Blood Count – This is used to determine the likelihood of anemia. Normal range is 4.10-5.60. The lower the result the more likely it is that the alcoholic is undernourished and has difficulty fighting off infection.

CREATININE, SERUM – To determine the functionality of the kidneys, a creatinine serum test will be performed. The levels will increase if the kidneys are not functioning normally. Normal range is 0.76-1.27.

POTASSIUM, SERUM – Most alcoholics are low on potassium which helps nerves and muscles communicate and aids in the flow of nutrients into cells and excretion of waste products. Low levels put the alcoholic in danger of a heart attack. Normal range is 3.5-5.2.

Use the results shown on the blood test to determine the progression of the alcoholic's bodily functions as shown on the lab report. A blank copy is on a separate page so that copies can be made to place into the workbook.

Lab Results Tracking Chart

Test	Jan	Feb	Mar	Apr	May	Jun	Jul	Aug	Sep	Oct	Nov	Dec
INR												
Prothrombin Time												
Ammonia, Plasma												
Magnesium, Serum												
RBC												
Creatinine, Serum												
Potassium, Serum												

LIVER FUNCTION TESTS

The following tests are used to determine liver function:

ALBUMIN, SERUM – Albumin is a protein made by the liver. It aids in keeping the blood flowing and prevents it from leaking into other tissues. Normal range is 3.6-4.8. A low result is an indication that the liver is not functioning properly.

BILIRUBIN, TOTAL – Bilirubin is the byproduct created from the older blood cells when they are replaced by newer ones. The liver breaks it down and the body excretes it in the stool. Bilirubin is what creates the yellowish color of the alcoholic's skin when not enough of it is excreted. Normal range is 0.1-1.2. A high result means there are too many older cells because the liver is not functioning property.

ALKALINE PHOSPHATASE – This is an enzyme that is produced in the liver primarily, but also in the bones, intestines and kidneys. A high score means the liver isn't functioning properly causing these enzymes to accumulate and block the bile ducts. Normal range is 25-160.

AST – Aspartate aminotransferase (AST) is an enzyme found in the liver, as well as the heart and other cells. A high score means the liver is damaged and is releasing this enzyme into the blood. Normal range is 0-40.

ALT – Alanine aminotransferase (ALT) is also an enzyme found in the liver and kidneys. A high result means these enzymes are being released into the blood and the liver is damaged. Normal range is 0-55.

Use the results shown on the blood test to determine the progression of the alcoholic's bodily functions as shown on the lab report. A blank copy is on a separate page so that copies can be made to place into the workbook.

Liver Function Tracking Chart

Test	Jan	Feb	Mar	Apr	May	June	July	Aug	Sept	Oct	Nov	Dec
Albumin, Serum												
Bilirubin, Total												
Alkaline Phosphatase												
AST												
ALT												

MELD AND CHILD-PUGH SCORES

See the sample lab report to understand where to get the correct numbers for the calculation charts. Enter in the chart the results circled in purple and labeled "MELD INFO" or "CHILD-PUGH INFO".

Meld Score

The MELD score is used by UNOS for determining the probability of life expectancy if a patient does not get a liver transplant. The information determines where the patient is placed on the liver waiting list. While most alcoholics do not meet the eligibility requirements for a liver transplant the same formula can be used to determine an anticipated life expectancy if the alcohol abuse does not stop. It is not an exact science and changes each time an alcoholic enters detox. However, it can give you an idea of how serious the condition is at any given point in time.

Add all three results together to get the MELD score. The interpretation is below:

A score of:

40 or more = 71.3% of people with this score die within three months

30-39 = 52.6% of people with this score die within three months

20-29 = 19.6% of people with this score die within three months

10-19 = 6.0% of people with this score die within three months

Less than 9 = 1.9% of people with this score die within three months

MELD SCORE CALCULATION CHART

Date	
Function	**Level**
Serum Bilirubin	
Serum Creatinine	
INR	
Total	
Meld Score	
Percentage	

CHILD-PUGH SCORE

This score is used in determining the possible life expectancy of one or two or more years of a person with liver disease. However, it uses two additional factors, **ASCITES** and **HEPATIC ENCEPHALOPATHY.**

Ascites

Ascites is a swelling in the stomach area due to an accumulation of fluid in the peritoneal cavity. It can also be accompanied with swelling in the ankles and legs. There are three classifications or grades:

Grade 1 =   Mild, only visible on ultrasound and CT

Grade 2 =   Detectable but not overtly obvious

Grade 3 =   Directly visible as similar to a "beer belly" or looking pregnant.

Hepatic Encephalopathy

Toxins from long term alcohol abuse lodge in the front lobe of the brain causing confusion, forgetfulness, irritability, inverted sleep patterns, tremors and difficulty with coordination. The worst case scenario is coma.

There are four grades used in determining the level of severity of the condition:

Grade 1 =   Slight lack of awareness; euphoria or anxiety; shortened attention span; impaired performance of addition or subtraction

Grade 2 =   Lethargy or apathy; some disorientation for time or place; subtle personality change; inappropriate behavior

Grade 3 =   Drowsiness; inverted sleep pattern; but responsive to verbal stimuli; confusion; gross disorientation

Grade 4 =   Coma (unresponsive)

SCORING

Refer to the lab reports to determine which point level is appropriate according to the following chart.

Function	1 point	2 points	3 points
Total bilirubin	Less than 2	2-3	More than 3
Serum albumin	More than 3.5	2.8-3.5	Less than 2.8
PT INR	Less than 1.7	1.71-2.20	More than 2.20
Ascites	Grade 1	Grade 2	Grade 3
Hepatic Encephalopathy	None	Grade 1 & 2	Grade 3 & 4

Class	Total points from scoring chart	One year survival	Two year survival
A	5-6	100%	85%
B	7-9	81%	57%
C	10-15	45%	35%

Child-Pugh Score Calculation Chart

Function	Points		
Total bilirubin			
Serum albumin			
Prothrombin time (INR)			
Ascities			
Hepatic Encephalopathy			
TOTAL POINTS			
CLASS			
One Year Survival Percentage		Two Year Survival Percentage	

See next page for the Record Chart.

Child Pugh Record Chart

Date	Points	Class	% Rate of Survival	
			One Year	Two Year

Sample Lab Reports

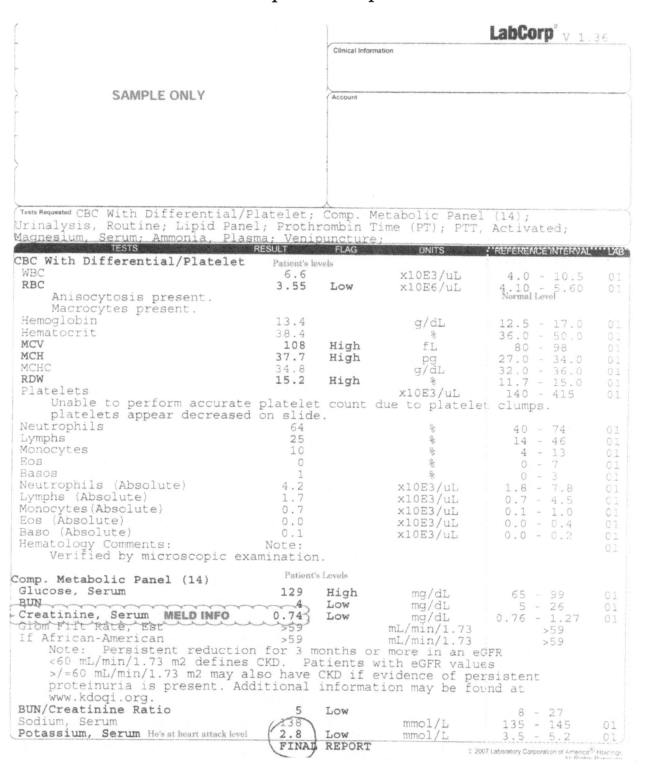

LabCorp® V 1.36

Clinical Information

Account

Tests Requested CBC With Differential/Platelet; Comp. Metabolic Panel (14);
Urinalysis, Routine; Lipid Panel; Prothrombin Time (PT); PTT, Activated;
Magnesium, Serum; Ammonia, Plasma; Venipuncture;

TESTS	RESULT	FLAG	UNITS	REFERENCE INTERVAL	LAB
CBC With Differential/Platelet	Patient's levels				
WBC	6.6		x10E3/uL	4.0 - 10.5	01
RBC	3.55	Low	x10E6/uL	4.10 - 5.60	01
Anisocytosis present.				Normal Level	
Macrocytes present.					
Hemoglobin	13.4		g/dL	12.5 - 17.0	01
Hematocrit	38.4		%	36.0 - 50.0	01
MCV	108	High	fL	80 - 98	01
MCH	37.7	High	pg	27.0 - 34.0	01
MCHC	34.8		g/dL	32.0 - 36.0	01
RDW	15.2	High	%	11.7 - 15.0	01
Platelets			x10E3/uL	140 - 415	01
Unable to perform accurate platelet count due to platelet clumps.					
platelets appear decreased on slide.					
Neutrophils	64		%	40 - 74	01
Lymphs	25		%	14 - 46	01
Monocytes	10		%	4 - 13	01
Eos	0		%	0 - 7	01
Basos	1		%	0 - 3	01
Neutrophils (Absolute)	4.2		x10E3/uL	1.8 - 7.8	01
Lymphs (Absolute)	1.7		x10E3/uL	0.7 - 4.5	01
Monocytes(Absolute)	0.7		x10E3/uL	0.1 - 1.0	01
Eos (Absolute)	0.0		x10E3/uL	0.0 - 0.4	01
Baso (Absolute)	0.1		x10E3/uL	0.0 - 0.2	01
Hematology Comments:	Note:				01
Verified by microscopic examination.					
Comp. Metabolic Panel (14)	Patient's Levels				
Glucose, Serum	129	High	mg/dL	65 - 99	01
BUN	4	Low	mg/dL	5 - 26	01
Creatinine, Serum MELD INFO	0.74	Low	mg/dL	0.76 - 1.27	01
Glom Filt Rate, Est	>59		mL/min/1.73	>59	
If African-American	>59		mL/min/1.73	>59	

Note: Persistent reduction for 3 months or more in an eGFR
<60 mL/min/1.73 m2 defines CKD. Patients with eGFR values
>/=60 mL/min/1.73 m2 may also have CKD if evidence of persistent
proteinuria is present. Additional information may be found at
www.kdoqi.org.

BUN/Creatinine Ratio	5	Low		8 - 27	
Sodium, Serum	138		mmol/L	135 - 145	01
Potassium, Serum He's at heart attack level	2.8	Low	mmol/L	3.5 - 5.2	01

FINAL REPORT

© 2007 Laboratory Corporation of America® Holdings.
All Rights Reserved.

Sample Lab Reports (Continued)

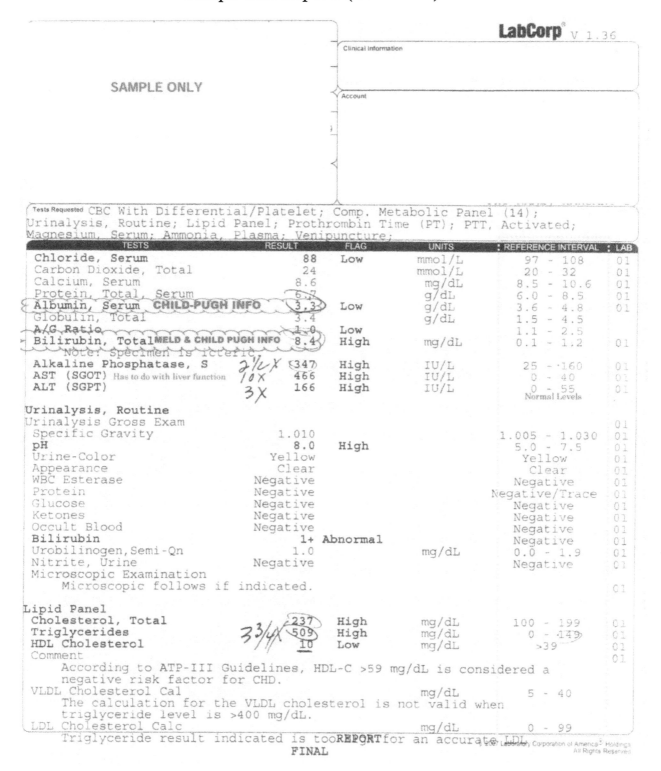

SAMPLE ONLY

LabCorp® V 1.36

Clinical Information

Account

Tests Requested CBC With Differential/Platelet; Comp. Metabolic Panel (14); Urinalysis, Routine; Lipid Panel; Prothrombin Time (PT); PTT, Activated; Magnesium, Serum; Ammonia, Plasma; Venipuncture;

TESTS	RESULT	FLAG	UNITS	REFERENCE INTERVAL	LAB
Chloride, Serum	88	Low	mmol/L	97 - 108	01
Carbon Dioxide, Total	24		mmol/L	20 - 32	01
Calcium, Serum	8.6		mg/dL	8.5 - 10.6	01
Protein, Total, Serum	6.7		g/dL	6.0 - 8.5	01
Albumin, Serum CHILD-PUGH INFO	3.3	Low	g/dL	3.6 - 4.8	01
Globulin, Total	3.4		g/dL	1.5 - 4.5	
A/G Ratio	1.0	Low		1.1 - 2.5	
Bilirubin, Total MELD & CHILD PUGH INFO	8.4	High	mg/dL	0.1 - 1.2	01
Note: Specimen is icteric					
Alkaline Phosphatase, S 2½X	347	High	IU/L	25 - 160	01
AST (SGOT) Has to do with liver function 10X	466	High	IU/L	0 - 40	01
ALT (SGPT) 3X	166	High	IU/L	0 - 55 Normal Levels	01
Urinalysis, Routine					
Urinalysis Gross Exam					01
Specific Gravity	1.010			1.005 - 1.030	01
pH	8.0	High		5.0 - 7.5	01
Urine-Color	Yellow			Yellow	01
Appearance	Clear			Clear	01
WBC Esterase	Negative			Negative	01
Protein	Negative			Negative/Trace	01
Glucose	Negative			Negative	01
Ketones	Negative			Negative	01
Occult Blood	Negative			Negative	01
Bilirubin	1+	Abnormal		Negative	01
Urobilinogen,Semi-Qn	1.0		mg/dL	0.0 - 1.9	01
Nitrite, Urine	Negative			Negative	01
Microscopic Examination					
Microscopic follows if indicated.					01
Lipid Panel					
Cholesterol, Total 3¾X	237	High	mg/dL	100 - 199	01
Triglycerides	509	High	mg/dL	0 - 149	01
HDL Cholesterol	10	Low	mg/dL	>39	01
Comment					01

According to ATP-III Guidelines, HDL-C >59 mg/dL is considered a negative risk factor for CHD.

| VLDL Cholesterol Cal | | | mg/dL | 5 - 40 | |

The calculation for the VLDL cholesterol is not valid when triglyceride level is >400 mg/dL.

| LDL Cholesterol Calc | | | mg/dL | 0 - 99 | |

Triglyceride result indicated is too **REPORT** for an accurate LDL. © Laboratory Corporation of America® Holdings All Rights Reserved.

FINAL

Sample Lab Reports (Continued)

LabCorp V 1.36

SAMPLE ONLY

Clinical Information

Account

Tests Requested CBC With Differential/Platelet; Comp. Metabolic Panel (14); Urinalysis, Routine; Lipid Panel; Prothrombin Time (PT); PTT, Activated; Magnesium, Serum; Ammonia, Plasma; Venipuncture;

TESTS	RESULT	FLAG	UNITS	REFERENCE INTERVAL	LAB
				Normal Levels	
cholesterol estimation.					
Prothrombin Time (PT)					
INR	1.1			0.8 - 1.2	01

Reference interval is for non-anticoagulated patients.

Suggested INR therapeutic range for Vitamin K antagonist therapy:
Standard Dose (moderate intensity

			therapeutic range):	2.0 - 3.0	
Higher intensity therapeutic range				2.5 - 3.5	
Prothrombin Time MELD & CHILD PUGH INFO 11.4			sec	8.7 - 11.5	01
PTT, Activated					
aPTT	29		sec	24 - 33	01

This test has not been validated for monitoring unfractionated heparin therapy. aPTT-based therapeutic ranges for unfractionated heparin therapy have not been established. For general guidelines on Heparin monitoring, refer to the LabCorp Directory of Services.

Magnesium, Serum	1.3	Low	mg/dL	1.6 - 2.6	01

This makes him mentally unstable

Ammonia, Plasma	497	Alert	ug/dL	27 - 102	01
Verified by repeat analysis				Normal Levels	

His liver is not breaking down the ammonia which should be released in his urine. The ammonia gets absorbed into his brain and acts as a poison.

01 SO   LabCorp San Diego   Dir: Kelli Hanson, MD
         13112 Evening Creek Dr So Ste 200, San Diego, CA 92128
For inquiries,the physician may contact **Branch: 800-859-6046 Lab: 858-668-3700**

LAST PAGE OF REPORT

Doctor's diagnosis *Hepatic Encephalopathy*

FINAL REPORT

© 2007 Laboratory Corporation of America Holdings

Based on the information on the sample lab report the following is the calculation for both MELD and Child-Pugh Scores:

MELD SCORE CALCULATION CHART

Date	
Function	**Level**
Serum Bilirubin	8.40
Serum Creatinine	.74
Prothrombin time (INR)	11.40
Total	20.54
Meld Score	20.54
Percentage	19.6%

From the information on the above chart, it can be determined that this patient has a 19.6% chance of surviving longer than three months from the date of the test.

CHILD-PUGH SCORE CALCULATION CHART

Function	Level	Points
Total bilirubin	8.4	3
Serum albumin	3.3	3
Prothrombin time (INR)	11.4	3
Ascities	2.0	2
Hepatic Encephalopathy	3.0	3
TOTAL POINTS		14
CLASS		C
One Year Survival		45%
Two Year Survival		35%

From the information on the above chart, it can be determined that this patient has a 45% chande of surviving longer than one year and 35% chance of surviving longer than two years from the date of the test.

THE TRUTH ABOUT DETOX

When an alcoholic has had many years of heavy drinking he must be admitted to the hospital and be closely monitored by medical professionals during the detoxification process. The reason for hospitalization is due to the risks involved. The truth about detox is:

1) The process itself creates a tremendous stress on the body which his heart may not be able to withstand. He may have a heart attack and / or a stroke. If he survives, he may have the same consequences of anyone else who has had a heart attack or stroke. Of course, in his weakened state he could very possibly die from the event.

2) Delirium Tremors may lead to seizures resulting in further brain damage, coma or death.

3) In the case of brain damage the effect could be minimal, but could also be substantial. He could lose the ability to use logic thinking, be easily confused, unable to function at an adult level, or at the extreme, leave him in a vegetative state.

4) He may wake up coherent and healthy, but he may have been in a black out for a portion or even his entire drinking time. He may not know where he is or why he is in the hospital. He may not recognize family members.

5) He will probably not remember the detox process so the event itself will not be a deterrent to future drinking.

6) Even if he decides to enter a rehabilitation program the odds are that he would most likely return to alcoholic drinking within 6 months of discharge.

Before the alcoholic goes into the hospital, there are no disclaimers issued. After the alcoholic is deep into the process (where you are at the point of no return), they tell you the truth. It comes out a bit at a time as you're watching the process progress.

For our family, we wondered if all the energy we expended trying to get him into the hospital was worth the uncertainty of the process. Had we insisted he go thru hell just to have a life he would find unbearable or no life at all?

In my opinion, the alcoholic is on a suicidal train – either from the drinking itself or the process to cleanse the alcohol from the body. Do the risks of detox outweigh the risks of continued drinking? The alcoholic cannot tell you because he lives in alcohol fog. The doctor can't tell you because he doesn't know what the end result will be. All the family knows is that they want this loved one to live a productive, healthy life – the family lives in Fantasyland.

So why do we hear everywhere that the best thing for an alcoholic is detox and rehab??

From the family point of view – any chance is better than no chance at all. The alcoholic is going to die one way or the other. With detox he at least has a chance for survival.

DETOXIFICATION HISTORY RECORD

Record any detoxification attempts in this workbook section. Start with the most recent and work backwards from there. Make copies of the blank records, if necessary, and add them to your workbook.

Dates Entered			Dated Exited			Completed Detox?		
Entered By	Voluntary			Court Ordered			Intervention	
Mental State	Conscious				Unconscious			
Transported via	Private Vehicle			Ambulance			Other	
Name of Center								
Address								
Phone Number								
Notes								

Dates Entered			Dated Exited			Completed Detox?		
Entered By	Voluntary			Court Ordered			Intervention	
Mental State	Conscious				Unconscious			
Transported via	Private Vehicle			Ambulance			Other	
Name of Center								
Address								
Phone Number								
Notes								

75

REHABILITATION HISTORY RECORDS

Record any drug and alcohol rehabilitation attempts in this workbook section. Start with the most recent and work backwards. Make copies of blank records and insert them in the workbook if more forms are needed.

Dates Entered		Dated Exited		Completed Program ?	
Entered By	Voluntary		Court Ordered		Intervention	
Resumed Drinking		How long after exiting did drinking resume			
Name of Center					
Address					
Phone Number					
Notes					

Dates Entered		Dated Exited		Completed Program ?	
Entered By	Voluntary		Court Ordered		Intervention	
Resumed Drinking		How long after exiting did drinking resume			
Name of Center					
Address					
Phone Number					
Notes					

Dates Entered		Dated Exited		Completed Program ?	
Entered By	Voluntary		Court Ordered		Intervention	
Resumed Drinking		How long after exiting did drinking resume			
Name of Center					
Address					
Phone Number					
Notes					

SUMMARY OF CONDITION

This is the section you will take with you to the doctor or medical facility. Put the Summary of Condition page on top and put the graphs behind it. The medical professional may not want the graphs, but this way they are easily eliminated. Make sure you give them a copy and not the original.

The graphs are a visual way of easily seeing whether the alcoholic is improving or declining. I'm a visual person and this is what works best for me. You may be happy with just the charts without the graphs or vice versa. It's your workbook and you can use it anyway you wish. I keep my Summary of Condition in the front cover of my binder. This lets me take it out for making changes.

Summary Of Condition Chart

Test	Jan	Feb	Mar	Apr	May	June	July	Aug	Sept	Oct	Nov	Dec
Overall Condition												
INR												
Prothrombin Time												
Ammonia, Plasma												
Magnesium, Serum												
RBC												
Creatinine, Serum												
Potassium, Serum												
Albumin, Serum												
Bilirubin, Total												
Alkaline Phosphatase												
AST (SGOT)												
ALT (SGPT)												
MELD												
Child-Pugh												

Summary Graphs

These charts will show the progression the alcoholic's condition.

Transfer the point values from the Summary of Condition Chart to the graph below by finding the point value in the column on the left and placing a line from the value in the first month to the value of the second month. Then continue to add lines from month to month.

Make a graph for each of the tests as shown on the Summary of Condition Chart. Use the same method transferring the information as in the Overall Condition chart below.

NOTE: To enter information onto this chart via your desktop, you must have a PDF program that allows editing (not just an a reader). See "How to Use This Workbook" for more information. If you don't have such a program, print out the form and use colored pencils or a highlighter to make your lines from value to value.

Overall Condition

	Jan	Feb	Mar	Apr	May	June	July	Aug	Sept	Oct	Nov	Dec
3												
4												
5												
6												
7												
8												
9												
10												
11												
12												
13												
14												
15												
16												
17												
18												
19												
20												
21												
22												
23												
24												

General Lab Results Chart

INR

	Jan	Feb	Mar	Apr	May	June	July	Aug	Sept	Oct	Nov	Dec
.08												
.09												
1.0												
1.1												
1.2												
1.4												
1.6												
1.8												
2.0												
2.2												
2.4												
2.6												
2.8												
2.9												
3.0												

Prothrombin Time

	Jan	Feb	Mar	Apr	May	June	July	Aug	Sept	Oct	Nov	Dec
11.2												
11.4												
11.6												
11.8												
12												
12.2												
12.4												
12.6												
12.8												
13												
13.2												
13.4												
13.6												
13.8												

Ammonia, Plasm

	Jan	Feb	Mar	Apr	May	June	July	Aug	Sept	Oct	Nov	Dec
102												
150												
200												
250												
300												
350												
400												
450												
500												
550												
600												
650												

RBC

	Jan	Feb	Mar	Apr	May	June	July	Aug	Sept	Oct	Nov	Dec
4.20												
4.10												
4												
3.80												
3.60												
3.40												
3.20												
3.10												
3												
2.80												
2.60												
2.40												
2.20												
2.10												
2												

Magnesium, Serum

	Jan	Feb	Mar	Apr	May	June	July	Aug	Sept	Oct	Nov	Dec
2.0												
1.6												
1.4												
1.2												
1												
.08												
.06												
.04												

Creatinine, Serum

	Jan	Feb	Mar	Apr	May	June	July	Aug	Sept	Oct	Nov	Dec
1.2												
.08												
.76												
.74												
.72												
.70												
.68												
.64												
.62												
.6												
.58												
.56												
.54												

Potassium, Serum

	Jan	Feb	Mar	Apr	May	June	July	Aug	Sept	Oct	Nov	Dec
4												
3.5												
3.4												
3.2												
3												
2.8												
2.6												
2.4												
2.2												
2												
1.8												
1.6												

Liver Function Tests Charts

Albumin, Serum

	Jan	Feb	Mar	Apr	May	June	July	Aug	Sept	Oct	Nov	Dec
4.0												
3.8												
3.6												
3.4												
3.2												
3												
2.8												
2.6												
2.4												
2.2												
2												
1.8												
1.6												
1.4												

Bilirubin, Total

	Jan	Feb	Mar	Apr	May	June	July	Aug	Sept	Oct	Nov	Dec
2.8												
3												
3.5												
4												
4.5												
5												
5.5												
6												
6.5												
7												
7.5												
8												
8.5												
9												
9.5												
10												

Alkaline Phosphatase

	Jan	Feb	Mar	Apr	May	June	July	Aug	Sept	Oct	Nov	Dec
180												
200												
250												
300												
350												
400												
450												
500												

AST (SGOT)

	Jan	Feb	Mar	Apr	May	June	July	Aug	Sept	Oct	Nov	Dec
50												
100												
150												
200												
250												
300												
350												
400												
450												
500												

ALT (SGPT)

	Jan	Feb	Mar	Apr	May	June	July	Aug	Sept	Oct	Nov	Dec
50												
55												
70												
80												
100												
150												
200												
250												
300												
350												
400												
450												
500												

Meld and Child Pugh Scores Charts

MELD

	Jan	Feb	Mar	Apr	May	June	July	Aug	Sept	Oct	Nov	Dec
40												
35												
30												
28												
26												
24												
22												
20												
18												
16												
14												
12												
10												
8												
6												

Child-Pugh Score (based on total points)

	Jan	Feb	Mar	Apr	May	June	July	Aug	Sept	Oct	Nov	Dec
6												
7												
9												
10												
11												
12												
13												
14												
16												

LEGAL STUFF

To simplify explanations the person signing the document and thereby giving authorization to make decisions on their behalf is called an AUTHORIZER. In our situation, in most cases, this person is usually the alcoholic. Because we caretakers need to have these documents for our own health care protection, I've chosen to use the "authorizer" term instead of just the "alcoholic."

The person that permission is being given to act in the interest of the authorizer is called the agent. So here is how it works:

AUTHORIZER   =   The one giving permission

AGENT   =   The one getting permission

The following information applies to both the alcoholic and the caretaker. Everyone should have these documents. For the caretaker, it determines who will make decisions about their care if the caretaker is unable to do so. In most states the responsibility falls to the spouse of the person who is incapacitated. If your spouse is an alcoholic, that may not be the person you want making decisions for you. Personally, my daughter has been made my agent in this event so that my husband will not have a part in deciding what happens to me. In certain cases, such as termination of life support, the decision requires a consensus of several people because I feel it is too heavy a burden for one person to carry.

Most alcoholics will be resistant to signing a legal document of any sort. In my opinion, the caretaker must do their best to get the documents signed. Wait for the most optimal moment – early in the morning worked best for me – and then attempt to have the conversation. Make sure you let the alcoholic know that the document can be amended or revoked at any time. It can also be set up to have an expiration date. Do whatever you can to make the prospect more appealing to the alcoholic and get the signature.

If you are a legal spouse, you may not need some of these documents in some states. But, having them simplifies things for everyone. For example, in the case of the Durable Power of Attorney, when I called the phone company to add an option, I discovered our account was only in my husband's name. If my husband was in the hospital or incapacitated, I would have had to send them a Durable Power of Attorney to show that I was authorized to make that change. Fortunately, my husband was right there and added me to the account without a problem. The situation could have been a huge issue requiring me to send proof that I was authorized to make changes to the account.

All of the documents may be amended or revoked. However, the authorizer must be mentally and physically capable of making that decision. For example, when Riley was going through detox, he tried to ban me from talking to the doctors. But, we had all the documents giving me permission to talk to them. It was deemed by the doctors and nurses that he was not in a mental state of mind to make such a decision. The documents held up to the test.

The various legal documents are described below and examples are at the end of this section. In the "Websites and References" Section, there are links to sites providing information concerning this documents.

The Advance Medical Directive

An Advance Medical Directive, also called a Health-care Proxy, makes the authorizer's wishes clear should he get to a point where he can no longer make medical decisions for himself. It relieves the caretaker of making the painful decision about whether or not to terminate life support, feeding tubes, etc. It sets out treatment preferences and designates a person to act as the decision-maker if the authorizer is unable to speak in his/her own behalf.

You may need assistance from your doctor or an attorney to fill out the form. But, in most cases, that isn't necessary. If you are unclear and don't want to seek outside help, just make sure to write out in your own words exactly what the authorizer wants and have him sign it. It does not require notarization. The document may be amended or revoked at any time.

This document can vary from state to state and can be obtained from your doctor's office, any hospital, or off the internet. I've included a copy at the end of this section.

Make several copies of this document and provide one for the medical records at your doctor's office and keep one in this workbook and the others in a safe place. Take one with you each time the alcoholic is admitted to a medical facility to be kept in the facility records.

The Living Will

This document is more specific in nature. Most commonly it includes a statement concerning termination of life-sustaining measures should the authorizer be deemed terminally ill without any hope of recovery. For example, if the authorizer goes into a coma and brain activity ceases, it grants permission to stop attempts to resuscitate. Generally, the patient is made comfortable with pain medication until the cessation of life.

However, this document can also specifically state what types of medication or activities may or may not be used to prolong life. They may include CPR, life-support equipment, feeding tubes, antibiotics, etc.

This form may be obtained from the doctor's office, any hospital or off the internet. I've include a sample form at the end of this section.

Make several copies of this document and provide one for the medical records at your doctor's office and keep several in this workbook. Take one with you each time the authorizer is admitted to a medical facility to be kept in those records.

This document may be amended or revoked at any time.

Durable Power of Attorney (DPOA)

A Durable Power of Attorney is a document that gives authorization for a person to represent the authorizer when he is incapacitated. It allows the agent to manage financial accounts, make health care decisions and make arrangements that the authorizer cannot because he/she is not in a position to do so for him/herself.

It is important that the agent be a person that the authorizer trusts to make decisions that benefit the authorizer. It should be a person close to the authorizer, a spouse, child, sibling or other family member. It can also be a close friend or even an attorney.

The person issuing the DPOA may put an expiration date on the document. For example, if the authorizer is going into rehab, the document can be valid from the date of entry to six months after admission. It can be amended or revoked at any time.

You may want to consult with an attorney before signing this document, but it is not absolutely necessary. It must be signed by the authorizer in the presence of a notary public and witnessed by an unbiased third person. Notary public's often come to you. Check your local phone book for one that provides this service.

Because of the powerful nature of this document, make several (10-12) originals, signed in blue ink to prevent mistaking it for a photocopy. Keep only one copy in this binder. Each time you sign something as an agent, you may have to provide an original DPOA. Keep extra originals in a safe place where you can easily get to them.

The Limited Durable Power of Attorney for Health Care

This is created only for health care and can do anything that a living will can do. The difference is that it gives the agent the power to actively remind the medical professionals of your wishes. The agent must follow the authorizer's wishes and can consider the physician's recommendations within reason. For example, if the authorizer is unconscious and bleeding internally, the doctor may recommend a blood transfusion. If the authorizer has made it known that he doesn't want any transfusions, the agent has the power to prevent the procedure. The same goes for other cases, such as surgery to repair bleeding ulcers. The agent has permission to give consent to the surgery. If the agent knows that the authorizer has asked for no surgery to be performed, the agent can decline the surgery.

Choosing an agent for this document should be done with careful consideration since there may be life and death issues at hand. The agent should be the person who knows the authorizer the best and has had discussions of what they would want if... It should also be someone who lives close by and can be present when decisions need to be made.

You may consult an attorney before signing this document, but it is not necessary. It is best to have the alcoholic's signature witnessed and notarized. The document may be amended or revoked at any time.

Make several photocopies of this document and provide one to your doctor's office for their records and keep several in this workbook. Take one with you each time the authorizer is admitted to a medical facility to be kept in those records. Just to be on the safe side, make a few originals, signed in blue ink, in case you are asked to produce an original. Keep a copy or an original in this binder, provide one to your doctor and take one with you to every medical facility.

It's Just My Opinion… but here's what I would do:

I've never had a problem getting Riley to sign documents. But, if he were resistant, this is what I would do –

1. Prepare all the documents for both of us and have them ready for signing before I start any conversation about them. Have a notary public and a witness lined up that can be at my house in a heart beat.

2. When Riley is the most coherent, I would tell him that someone we both know recently went through a situation where one spouse could not stop a procedure (or authorize a procedure) that was necessary to saving the person's life. If I can personalize the story – it might strike a spark of understanding on Riley's part.

3. I'd tell Riley that the situation got me thinking about what would happen if something were to happen to me and I were unable to make a decision about my care. This way I'm turning the focus off him and onto me. I'd tell him I just want to make sure he knows what I want in case the worst things happen.

4. I'd explain to Riley what my desires would be. Then tell him I've put together some documents that I'm going to sign to give him permission to take care of me. *Stop freaking out – I'll fix it all at the end.*

5. After talking about what I would want – I'd ask what Riley would want. Turn the tables and focus on he wants and desires. I'd tell him, it would help if he would sign the same documents that I'm signing. I'd make sure to tell him that the documents may be amended or revoked at any time and there is a form that would do that which would be kept with the documents. He can sign it whenever he feels that I'm not acting in his best interest.

6. I'd make sure to tell Riley that the documents can state that he does not want to be placed in a rehab center unless he, personally, requests the placement.

7. As soon as Riley agrees to the signing, I'd call the notary public and witness and get them there pronto.

8. This part is extremely important: After the documents are safely signed and a day, week or just after a bit of time has passed, I would write up a new set of documents covering **me** only. I would not write up new documents for Riley. I'd be sure that they state these new documents (pertaining to me) supersede any previously signed documents which are now null and void. Have all the documents notarized and witnessed. I would include a separate document that makes a statement that on that date, I am declaring any and all previously signed documents (list them by their appropriate names) are now revoked and that they are all now null and void. This is my protection from having the alcoholic determine your health or any other decisions for me.

9. DO NOT TELL THE ALCOHOLIC THAT YOU HAVE REVOKED HIS POWER. Getting into a discussion about the documents after the signing is not in your best interest. If the alcoholic is truly end-stage, they will, most likely, forget about it and not bring it up again.

Advance Health Care Directive Form Instructions

SAMPLE
Advance Health Care Directive Form Instructions

You have the right to give instructions about your own health care.

You also have the right to name someone else to make health care decisions for you.

The Advance Health Care Directive Form lets you do one or both of these things. It also lets you write down your wishes about donation of organs and the selection of your primary physician. If you use the form, you may complete or change any part of it or all of it. You are free to use a different form.

INSTRUCTIONS

Part 1: Power of Attorney

Part 1 lets you:

- **name** another person as **agent** to make health care decisions for you if you are unable to make your own decisions. You can also have your agent make decisions for you right away, even if you are still able to make your own decisions.

- **also name** an **alternate agent** to act for you if your first choice is not willing, able or reasonably available to make decisions for you.

Your **agent** may not be:

- an operator or employee of a community care facility or a residential care facility where you are receiving care.

- your supervising health care provider (the doctor managing your care)

- an employee of the health care institution where you are receiving care, unless your agent is related to you or is a coworker.

Your **agent** may make all health care decisions for you, unless you limit the authority of your agent. You do not need to limit the authority of your agent.

If you want to limit the authority of your agent the form includes a place where you can limit the authority of your agent.

If you choose not to limit the authority of your agent, your agent will have the right to:

- Consent or refuse consent to any care, treatment, service, or procedure to maintain, diagnose, or otherwise affect a physical or mental condition.

- Choose or discharge health care providers (i.e. choose a doctor for you) and institutions.

- Agree or disagree to diagnostic tests, surgical procedures, and medication plans.

- Agree or disagree with providing, withholding, or withdrawal of artificial feeding and fluids and all other forms of health care, including cardiopulmonary resuscitation (CPR).

- After your death make anatomical gifts (donate organs/tissues), authorize an autopsy, and make decisions about what will be done with your body.

Part 2: Instructions for Health Care

You can give specific instructions about any aspect of your health care, whether or not you appoint an agent.

There are choices provided on the form to help you write down your wishes regarding providing, withholding or withdrawal of treatment to keep you alive.

You can also add to the choices you have made or write out any additional wishes.

You do not need to fill out part 2 of this form if you want to allow your agent to make any decisions about your health care that he/she believes best for you without adding your specific instructions.

111

Part 3: Donation of Organs

You can write down your wishes about donating your bodily organs and tissues following your death.

Part 4: Primary Physician

You can select a physician to have primary or main responsibility for your health care.

Part 5: Signature and Witnesses

After completing the form, **sign and date it** in the section provided.

The form must be signed **by two qualified witnesses** (see the statements of the witnesses included in the form) **or** acknowledged before a notary public. **A notary is not required if the form is signed by two witnesses. The wittnesses must sign the form on the same date it is signed by the person making the Advance Directive.**

See part 6 of the form if you are a patient in a skilled nursing facility.

Part 6: Special Witness Requirement

A Patient Advocate or Ombudsman must witness the form *if you are a patient in a skilled nursing facility* (a health care facility that provides skilled nursing care and supportive care to patients). See Part 6 of the form.

You have the right to change or revoke your Advance Health Care Directive at any time

If you have questions about completing the Advance Directive in the hospital, please ask to speak to a Chaplain or Social Worker.

We ask that you
complete this form in English
so your caregivers can understand your directions.

Advance Health Care Directive

SAMPLE
Advance Health Care Directive

Name_____

Date_____

You have the right to give instructions about your own health care. You also have the right to name someone else to make health care decisions for you. This form also lets you write down your wishes regarding donation of organs and the designation of your primary physician. If you use this form, you may complete or change all or any part of it. You are free to use a different form.

You have the right to change or revoke this advance health care directive at any time.

Part 1 — Power of Attorney for Health Care

(1.1) DESIGNATION OF AGENT: I designate the following individual as my agent to make health care decisions for me:

Name of individual you choose as agent:_____

Relationship_____

Address: _____

_____

Telephone numbers: (Indicate home, work, cell) _____

ALTERNATE AGENT (Optional): If I revoke my agent's authority or if my agent is not willing, able, or reasonably available to make a health care decision for me, I designate as my first alternate agent:

Name of individual you choose as alternate agent:_____

Relationship_____

Address: _____

_____

Telephone numbers: (Indicate home, work, cell) _____

SECOND ALTERNATE AGENT (optional): If I revoke the authority of my agent and first alternate agent or if neither is willing, able, or reasonably available to make a health care decision for me, I designate as my second alternate agent:

Name of individual you choose as second alternate agent:_____

Address: _____

_____

Telephone numbers: (Indicate home, work, cell) _____

(1.2) AGENT'S AUTHORITY: My agent is authorized to 1) make all health care decisions for me, including decisions to provide, withhold, or withdraw artificial nutrition and hydration and all other forms of health care to keep me alive, 2) to choose a particular physician or health care facility, and 3) to receive or consent to the release of medical information and records, except as I state here:

_____

_____

(Add additional sheets if needed.)

(1.3) WHEN AGENT'S AUTHORITY BECOMES EFFECTIVE: My agent's authority becomes effective when my primary physician determines that I am unable to make my own health care decisions unless I initial the following line.

If I initial this line, my agent's authority to make health care decisions for me takes effect immediately. ____

(1.4) AGENT'S OBLIGATION: My agent shall make health care decisions for me in accordance with this power of attorney for health care, any instructions I give in Part 2 of this form, and my other wishes to the extent known to my agent. To the extent my wishes are unknown, my agent shall make health care decisions for me in accordance with what my agent determines to be my best interest. In determining my best interest, my agent shall consider my personal values to the extent known to my agent.

(1.5) AGENT'S POST DEATH AUTHORITY: My agent is authorized to make anatomical gifts, authorize an autopsy, and direct disposition of my remains, except as I state here or in Part 3 of this form:

_____

(Add additional sheets if needed.)

(1.6) NOMINATION OF CONSERVATOR: If a conservator of my person needs to be appointed for me by a court, I nominate the agent designated in this form. If that agent is not willing, able, or reasonably available to act as conservator, I nominate the alternate agents whom I have named. _____ (initial here)

Part 2 — Instructions for Health Care

If you fill out this part of the form, you may strike out any wording you do not want.

(2.1) **END-OF-LIFE DECISIONS**: I direct my health care providers and others involved in my care to provide, withhold, or withdraw treatment in accordance with the choice I have marked below:

☐ a) Choice Not To Prolong
   I do not want my life to be prolonged if the likely risks and burdens of treatment would outweigh the expected benefits, or if I become unconscious and, to a realistic degree of medical certainty, I will not regain consciousness, or if I have an incurable and irreversible condition that will result in my death in a relatively short time.
   Or
☐ b) Choice To Prolong
   I want my life to be prolonged as long as possible within the limits of generally accepted medical treatment standards.

FIRST WITNESS

Print Name: _____

Address: _____

Signature of Witness: _____ Date: _____

SECOND WITNESS

Print Name: _____

Address: _____

Signature of Witness: _____ Date: _____

(5.4) ADDITIONAL STATEMENT OF WITNESSES: At least one of the above witnesses must also sign the following declaration:

I further declare under penalty of perjury under the laws of California that I am not related to the individual executing this advance directive by blood, marriage, or adoption, and to the best of my knowledge, I am not entitled to any part of the individual's estate on his or her death under a will now existing or by operation of law.

Signature of Witness: _____

Signature of Witness: _____

Part 6 — Special Witness Requirement if in a Skilled Nursing Facility

(6.1) The patient advocate or ombudsman must sign the following statement:

STATEMENT OF PATIENT ADVOCATE OF OMBUDSMAN

I declare under penalty of perjury under the laws of California that I am a patient advocate or ombudsman as designated by the State Department of Aging and that I am serving as a witness as required by section 4675 of the Probate Code:

Print Name:_____ Signature: _____

Address: _____ Date: _____

Certificate of Acknowledgement of Notary Public (Not required if signed by two witnesses)

State of California, County of _____ On this _____ day of

_____ , _____ , before me, the undersigned, a Notary Public in and for

said State, personally appeared _____ , personally known to me or

proved to me on the basis of satisfactory evidence to be the person whose name is subscribed to the

within instrument, and acknowledged _____

to me that he/she executed it.

WITNESS my hand an official seal. Seal

Signature_____

Sample Living Will Form

SAMPLE

ILLNESS & HOSPITALIZATION

SAMPLE LIVING WILL FORM

Each of the fifty states have some law regarding the ability of patients to make decisions about their medical care before the need for treatment arises through the use of advance directives. The great majority of states allow for patients to draft living wills that set forth the type and duration of medical care that they wish to receive should they become unable to communicate those wishes on their own.

Although the law in each state will vary as to what can be included in a living will, the following sample can provide a general overview of what one may look like, and what information may be included. **Of course, before assuming that this sample will be sufficient for your purposes, you should check the law in your jurisdiction or have an attorney review your advance directives.** In some states, however, an unapproved document may have some persuasive effect.

LIVING WILL DECLARATION OF _____

To my family, doctors, hospitals, surgeons, medical care providers, and all others concerned with my care:

I, _____, being of sound mind and rational thought willfully and voluntarily make this declaration to be followed if I become incompetent or incapacitated to the extent that I am unable to communicate my wishes, desires and preferences on my own.

This declaration reflects my firm, informed, and settled commitment to refuse life-sustaining medical care and treatment under the circumstances that are indicated below.

This declaration and the following directions are an expression of my legal right to refuse medical care and treatment. I expect and trust the above-mentioned parties to regard themselves as legally and morally bound to act in accordance with my wishes, desires, and preferences. The above-mentioned parties should therefore be free from any legal liabilities for having followed this declaration and the directions that it contains.

DIRECTIONS

1. I direct my attending physician or primary care physician to withhold or withdraw life-sustaining medical care and treatment that is serving only to prolong the process of my dying if I should be in an incurable or irreversible mental or physical condition with no reasonable medical expectation of recovery.

2. I direct that treatment be limited to measures which are designed to keep me comfortable and to relieve pain, including any pain which might occur from the withholding or withdrawing of life-sustaining medical care or treatment.

3. I direct that if I am in the condition described in item 1, above, it be remembered that I specifically **do not** want the following forms of medical care and treatment:

   A. _____
   B. _____

C. _____
D. _____
E. _____
F. _____
G. _____
H. _____
I. _____
J. _____
K. _____

4. I direct that if I am in the condition described in item 1, above, it be remembered that I specifically **do** want the following forms of medical care and treatment:

A. _____
B. _____
C. _____
D. _____
E. _____
F. _____
G. _____
H. _____
I. _____
J. _____
K. _____

5. I direct that if I am in the condition described in item 1, above, and if I also have the condition or conditions of _____, that I receive the following medical care and treatment:

_____
_____
_____
_____
_____
_____
_____
_____
_____

This Living Will Declaration expresses my firm wishes, desires, and preferences and the fact that I may have executed a form specified by the law of the State of _____, may not be used a limiting or contradicting this Living Will Declaration, which is an expression of both my common law and constitutional rights.

I make this Living Will Declaration the _____ day of _____, 20____.

_____
Declarant's Signature

_____
_____
Declarant's Address

WITNESS STATEMENTS

I declare that the person who signed or acknowledged this document is personally known to me, that he/she signed or acknowledged this Living Will Declaration in my presence, and that he/she appears to be of sound mind and under no duress, fraud, or undue influence.

_____

Witnesses' Signature

_____

Witnesses' Printed Name

_____

Witnesses' Address

I declare that the person who signed or acknowledged this document is personally known to me, that he/she signed or acknowledged this Living Will Declaration in my presence, and that he/she appears to be of sound mind and under no duress, fraud, or undue influence.

_____

Witnesses' Signature

_____

Witnesses' Printed Name

_____

_____

Witnesses' Address

NOTARIZATION

STATE OF _____, COUNTY OF _____

Subscribed and sworn to before me his _____ day of _____, 20_____.

_____

Signature of Notary Public

My commission expires: _____

NOTES ABOUT LIVING WILL DECLARATION FORM:

- Paragraphs one and two can be tailored to suit your own desires. For example, you could redraft paragraph one to state that you would like to have life-sustaining treatments for "x" number of days or weeks and then if no progress is made and there is no reasonable hope of recovery, you would like to have the life-sustaining treatments withdrawn. As for paragraph two, if you do not wish to receive pain medications you can state those wishes there.

- Paragraph three of the Declaration allows you to list all specific types of treatment you wish not to receive. If you do not have strong feelings about any particular types of treatment, you do not need to include this paragraph in your own living will. However, if you do have strong preferences, this is the place to list them.

    Examples: Antibiotics, artificial feedings, hydration and fluids, blood transfusions, cardiac resuscitation, dialysis, intravenous lines, invasive tests, respiratory therapy, mechanical respiratory assistance, and surgery.

    Note: For many people, taking away food and water from a dying person seems especially cruel because they may feel as though the person is starving or dehydrating to death. However, you have a right to make your specific wishes known on the subject. It is advisable, however, to be particularly clear on those issues so that there is no room for your loved ones to debate. In addition, they will likely feel less burdened by guilt if they are certain they are following your specific wishes not to be artificially fed or hydrated.

- Paragraph four is the converse of paragraph three and allows you to clearly state what care and treatment you would like to receive. In addition, if you have specific instructions for other types of care, you may wish to include them in this paragraph.

    Examples: At-home or hospice care as the end approaches, feelings about religious practices or customs at a terminal stage (for instance, if you wish for a certain clergy member to be called and be present).

- Paragraph six allows you to essentially "change" your wishes should you also have another medical condition when you become incapacitated or incompetent.

    Example: For women of child-bearing age, the desire to forego life-sustaining treatment may be compromised if they are pregnant. In those situations, they may wish to be kept alive, if possible, until the baby can be safely delivered at which point, if there has been no recovery or reasonable progress, they may wish to then have their life-sustaining treatments withdrawn.

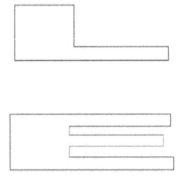

Sample Durable Power of Attorney

SAMPLE

Sample Power of Attorney Form

POWER OF ATTORNEY

KNOW ALL MEN BY THESE PRESENTS:

[Individual], hereinafter referred to as PRINCIPAL, in the County of _____ State of _____, being of sound mind, do(es) appoint [individual] as his (her) true and lawful attorney-in-fact.

Any and all general powers of attorney that previously have been signed by principal are hereby revoked. However, the preceding sentence shall not have the effect of revoking any powers of attorney that are directly related to principal's health care that previously have been signed by principal.

In the principal's name, and for the principal's use and benefit, said attorney-in-fact is authorized hereby:

(1) Sell, exchange, buy, invest, or reinvest any assets or property owned, which may include income producing or non-income producing assets and property.

(2) Open, maintain or close bank accounts (including, but not limited to, checking accounts, savings accounts, and certificates of deposit), brokerage accounts, and other similar accounts with financial institutions.

(a) Conduct any business with any banking or financial institution with respect to any of principal's accounts, including, but not limited to, making deposits and withdrawals, obtaining bank statements, passbooks, drafts, money orders, warrants, and certificates or vouchers payable to the principal by any person, firm, corporation or political entity.

(b) Perform any act necessary to deposit, negotiate, sell or transfer any note, security, or draft of the United States of America, including U.S. Treasury Securities.

(c) Have access to any safe deposit box owned, including its contents.

(3) Take any and all legal steps necessary to collect any amount or debt owed, or to settle any claim, whether made against or asserted on behalf of principal against any other person or entity.

(4) Exercise all stock rights as proxy, including all rights with respect to stocks, bonds, debentures, or other investments.

(5) Maintain and/or operate any business owned by principal.

(6) Purchase and / or maintain insurance

(7) Enter into binding contracts on behalf of principal

(8) Employ professional and business assistance as may be appropriate

(9) Sell, convey, lease, mortgage, manage, insure, improve, repair, or perform any other act with respect to any of principal's property currently owned or acquired later, including, but not limited to, real estate and real estate rights (including the right to remove tenants and to recover possession). This includes the right to sell or encumber any homestead currently owned or may own in the future.

(10) Transfer any of principal's assets to the trustee of any revocable trust created by principal, if such trust is in existence at the time of such transfer.

(11) Prepare, sign, and file documents with any governmental body or agency, including, but not limited to, authorization to:

(a) Prepare, sign and file income and other tax returns with federal, state, local, and other governmental bodies.

(b) Obtain information or documents from any government or its agencies, and negotiate, compromise, or settle any matter with such government or agency (including tax matters).

(c) Prepare applications, provide information, and perform any other act reasonably requested by any government or its agencies in connection with governmental benefits (including military and social security benefits).

(12) Make gifts from assets to members of family and to such other persons or charitable organizations with whom principal has an established pattern of giving. However, said attorney may not make gifts of principal's property to the said attorney. The Principal hereby appoints _____, of _____ _____, as substitute Agent for the sole purpose of making gifts of property to said attorney, as deemed appropriate.

(13) Disclaim any interest that might otherwise be transferred or distributed to principal from any other person, estate, trust, or other entity, as may be appropriate.

Said attorney-in-fact shall not be liable for any loss that results from a judgment error that was made in good faith. However, said attorney shall be liable for willful misconduct or the failure to act in good faith while acting under the authority of this Power of Attorney.

Principal authorizes said attorney to indemnify and hold harmless any third party who accepts and acts under this document.

Giving and granting to said attorney full power and authority to do all and every act and thing whatsoever requisite and necessary to be done relative to any of the foregoing as fully to all intents and purposes as principal might or could do if personally present.

All that said attorney shall lawfully do or cause to be done under the authority of this power of attorney is expressly approved.

[If witnesses are required, the following must be included:
WITNESS' SIGNATURE: _____

WITNESS' PRINTED FULL LEGAL NAME: _____

WITNESS' SIGNATURE: _____

WITNESS' PRINTED FULL LEGAL NAME: _____]

Dated: _____, 20_____ at _____, _____.

By: _____

STATE OF _____ COUNTY OF _____

BEFORE ME, the undersigned authority, on this _____ day of _____, 20_____, personally appeared _____ to me well known to be the person described in and who signed the foregoing, and acknowledged to me that he executed the same freely and voluntarily for the uses and purposes therein expressed.

WITNESS my hand and official seal the date aforesaid.

NOTARY PUBLIC

My Commission Expires:

Sample Durable Health Care Power of Attorney

STATE OF
ALABAMA   )

)   **SAMPLE**

COUNTY OF   )

DURABLE HEALTH CARE POWER OF ATTORNEY

KNOW ALL MEN BY THESE PRESENTS THAT I, _____, of _____, City of _____, County of _____, Alabama, hereby make, constitute and appoint _____, whose address is _____, to act as my agent or attorney in fact, to make health care and related personal decisions for me as authorized in this document. Should _____ for any reason be unable or unwilling to act, temporarily or permanently, then I appoint _____, of _____, as such agent/attorney in fact, with the same authority.

By this document I intend to create a durable power of attorney upon, and only during, any period of incapacity in which, in the opinion of my health care agent/attorney in fact, after consultation with my health care providers, I am unable to make or communicate a choice regarding a particular health care decision. This document is intended to complement and supplement any Advance Health Care Directive and/or Durable Power of Attorney for financial matters that I may have executed or may execute in the future. It is my desire to receive appropriate medical treatment so long as there is a reasonable hope of recovery, but I do not want my life artificially extended beyond any reasonable hope of recovery to a meaningful quality of life and I do not want to prolong the dying process. I do not intend by this document to authorize or request euthanasia or assisted suicide but to avoid being unwillingly sustained in a condition that is only a semblance of life; or to be allowed to endure pain for which there is treatment available, whether or not recovery is possible.

I grant to my agent full power to make decisions for me regarding my health care. In exercising his/her authority, my agent shall attempt to communicate with me regarding my wishes if I am able to communicate in any way. If my agent cannot determine the choice I want made, then (s)he shall make the choice for me based upon what (s)he believes I would do if I were able, or if unable to so determine, then based upon what (s)he believes to be my best interests. I intend the power given to be as broad as possible, except for any limitations in my Advance Directives or set out hereinafter. Accordingly, unless so limited, my agent is authorized:

To consent to, refuse or withdraw consent to any and all types of medical care, treatment, surgical procedures, diagnostic procedures, medications and use of mechanical or other procedures affecting bodily functions; including, without limitation, artificial respiration, nutritional support and hydration, and cardiopulmonary resuscitation;

- To have access to and have the right to disclose medical reports, records and information to the extent that I would myself;
- To authorize admission to or discharge from any hospital, residential care or related facility, even against medical advice;
- To contract for health care or related services, without the agent incurring personal liability therefore;
- To hire and fire medical, social service or related personnel responsible for my care;
- To authorize or refuse to authorize any medication or procedure to relieve pain, even though such use may lead to temporary discomfort or addiction, or inadvertently hasten the moment of death;
- To make anatomical gifts of part of all of my body for medical purposes,
- To authorize an autopsy and direct disposition of my remains, to the extent permitted by law, and
- To take any other action necessary to effectuate the intent and purpose of this broad grant of powers, including, without limitation, granting any waiver of release from liability required by any health care provider or related agency, and
- To sign any document relative to health care in any way whatsoever and pursuing legal action in my

name at the expense of my estate, should that be necessary to enforce compliance with my wishes as determined by my agent pursuant to the authority given herein.

Without in any way limiting the broad powers herein granted, I express the hope that, circumstances permitting, my agent will consult family and friends for their advice and support in arriving at what may be difficult decisions; but the final decisions shall be that of my agent.

No person who relies in good faith upon any representation of my agent or successor agent shall be liable to me, my estate, my heirs or assignees, for recognizing the agent's authority. Although no compensation of my agent is contemplated, (s)he shall be entitled to reimbursement of any and all reasonable expenses incurred as a result of carrying out any provision of this document.

Invalidity of one or more powers shall not invalidate any others.

I am in full control of my mental faculties and I understand the contents of this document and the effect of this grant of powers to my agent.

Dated this _____ day of _____, 201__ .

_____,Grantor

WITNESSES

I believe the Grantor to be of sound mind and able to make decisions of this kind. I did not sign his/her name and I am not the health care agent. I am not related to the Grantor by blood, adoption or marriage, and not entitled to any part of his/her estate. I am at least 19 years old and am not directly responsible for his/her medical care or expenses.

_____
Signature of Witness

_____
Name of Witness

Date: _____

and

_____
Signature of Witness

_____
Name of Witness

Date: _____

ATTESTATION

I, the undersigned authority in and for said County in said State, hereby certify that _____, whose name is signed to the foregoing Durable Health Care Power of Attorney, and who is known to me, acknowledged before me on this day that, being informed of the contents of the said document, (s)he executed the same voluntarily, before the witnesses whose names appear above, on the day the same bears date.

Given under my hand this _____ day of _____, 2002.

_____
Notary Public

My commission expires:

_____

SIGNATURES OF AGENTS

I, _____, am willing to serve as Health Care Agent.

Signature: _____ Date: _____

I, _____, am willing to serve as Health Care Agent if the first-named Agent cannot serve.

Signature: _____ Date: _____

WEBSITES AND REFERENCES

I have found the following websites to be instrumental in obtaining information.

GENERAL INFORMATION:

1. www.nlm.nih.gov

2. http://www.emedicinehealth.com/alcoholism/article_em.htm

3. http://www.ncbi.nlm.nih.gov/books?term=alcoholism

4. www.pubs.niaaa.nih.gov

5. http://en.wikipedia.org/wiki/alcoholism

6. http://www.ehow.com/about_5041054_symptoms-end-stage-alcoholism.html

7. http://www.alcoholism-facts.com/end-stage-alcoholism.php

8. www.recoverymonth.gov

SUPPORT SITES, FORUMS and BLOGS:

9. www.immortalalcoholic.blogspot.com

10. https://www.facebook.com/groups/273999545981419/283233241724716/?ref=notif&notif_t=group_activity#!/groups/273999545981419/283233241724716/?notif_t=group_activity

11. http://www.nursepractioner.org/addiction-blogs

12. http://www.hypercryptical.blogspot.com/

13. http://www.alcoholicdaze.blogspot.com/

14. http://fine-anon.blogspot.com/

15. http://texandave.blogspot.com/

16. http://gerry-daughters-of-the-shadow-men-ii.blogspot.com/

17. www.sober.com

18. www.community.aetv.com

19. http://www.the-alcoholism-guide.org/alcoholism-questions.html

20. http://www.thriveinlife.ca/thrive

21. www.al-anon.org

22. www.aa.org

23. www.alcoholism.com

24. www.alcoholism.about.com

25. www.recoverymonth.gov

MEDICAL INFO:

26.   www.webmd.com

27.   www.pubs.niaaa.nih.gov

28.   http://en.wikipedia.org/wiki/alcoholism

29.   http://www.the-alcoholism-guide.org/alcoholism-questions.html

30.   http://www.egetgoing.com/Drug/5_9_2_1_2.asp

31.   http://www.ehow.com/about_5041054_symptoms-end-stage-alcoholism.html

32.   http://www.alcoholism-facts.com/end-stage-alcoholism.php

33.   http://providentliving.org/pfw/multimedia/files/pfw/pdf/122750_15BPHLR_pdf.pdf

34.   www.fsis.usda.gov/factsheets/parasites_and...**illness**/index.asp

35.   www.en.wikipedia.org/wiki/**Human_feces**

36.   www.en.wikipedia.org/wiki/**Human_waste**

LEGAL STUFF:

37.   http://www.caringinfo.org/i4a/pages/index.cfm?pageid=3289

38.   http://ag.ca.gov/consumers/pdf/AHCDS1.pdf

39.   http://www.medicinenet.com/script/main/art.asp?articlekey=46355

40.   http://www.doyourownwill.com/living-will/states.html

41.   http://estate.findlaw.com/estate-planning/living-wills/le23_9_1.html

42.   http://www.expertlaw.com/library/estate_planning/durable_power_of_attorney.html

43.   http://www.uaelderlaw.org/advance/7.html

44.   http://www.clearleadinc.com/site/power-of-attorney-form.html

EXTRA FORMS

On the following pages you will find forms for you to photocopy and place into your binder workbook.

Doctor's Appointment Forms

The "Information for Doctor's Appointment" form is not included in the body of the book. It's what I use whenever I take Riley to the doctor. It simplifies explanations and keeps the appointment on track.

For a first time visit make sure to also take the General Information, Medical History, Family History, Current/Ongoing Conditions and Resolved Conditions forms as well. This will keep you from having to fill out all that paperwork while in the doctor's office.

I also use these forms for my own personal health information.

Information for Doctor's Appointment

Name of Patient Address and Phone Number of Patient

CURRENT ISSUES / CONCERNS

(Why are you seeing the doctor today?)

Issues	Comments

RECENT TREATMENTS

Start	End	Treatment

CURRENT MEDICATION LIST

Medication	Dosage	Frequency	For

RECENT MEDICAL TESTING

	Recent Testing

MEDICAL HISTORY

Year	Diagnosis	Comments

HOSPITALIZATIONS

Year	Diagnosis	Hospital

Basic Information

NAME OF ALCOHOLIC				
CURRENT AGE			BIRTHDATE	
DAILY CONSUMPTION (Liters - LT / Ounces - OZ)		DRINK OF CHOICE		
LAST DAY OF SOBRIETY		AGE AT FIRST DRINK		
NUMBER OF TIMES IN DETOX		NUMBER OF TIMES IN REHAB		
LAST DETOX FACILITY NAME				
Date of Admittance		Phone Number		
Address				
Notes				
LAST REHAB CENTER NAME				
Date of Admittance		Phone Number		
Address				
Notes				
CARETAKERS NAME, Relationship				
EMERGENCY CONTACT NAME, Relationship				
Emergency Contact Phone Number		Other / Cell		
SECONDARY CONTACT NAME, Relationship				
Secondary Phone Number		Other / Cell		
INTERNIST / PHYSICIAN NAME				
Internist / Physician Contact Info				
THERAPIST/COUNSELOR NAME				
Therapist/Counselor Contact Info				
OTHER CONTACT INFO				
Contact Phone Number		Other / Cell		
OTHER ILLNESS / CONDITIONS				
Date of Onset				
Prognosis				
OTHER ILLNESS / CONDITION				
Date of Onset				
Prognosis				
PRIMARY MEDICAL INSURANCE				
Policy Number / Group Number Information				
SECONDARY MEDICAL INSURANCE				
Policy Number / Group Number Information				

Medical History

On the next page you will find a chart for indicating any diagnosis of previous conditions that the patient may have been treated in the past.

NOTE: All forms are included at the end of the book where it can be removed and photocopied allowing it to be inserted into a binder.

Condition	Current	Resolved
Anemia		
Arthritis		
Asthma / Allergies		
Bleeding Problems		
Cancer		
Cirrhosis		
Delirium Tremens		
Dementia		
Diabetes		
Epilepsy		
Esophageal Bleeding		
Gastritis / Ulcers		
Glaucoma		
Heart Disease / Issues		
Hepatic Encephalopathy		
Hepatitis		
High Cholesterol		
Hypertension / High Blood Pressure		
Kidney Diseases		
Migraine Headaches		
Oriental Flushing Syndrome		
Osteoarthritis		
Osteoporosis		
Pancreatitis		
Polyneuropathy / Neurological Issues		
Rheumatoid Arthritis		
Stroke		
Thyroid Disorders		
Vision Issues		
Wernicke-Korsakoff		
OTHER:		

Current / On-Going Conditions

Condition	Date diagnosed	Date Lasted treated	Notes / Prognosis

Resolved Conditions

Condition	Date diagnosed	Date Lasted treated	Notes / Prognosis

Family History

Relative	Living	Health Issues	Deceased (mo/yr)	Cause of death
Father				
Mother				
Sibling (M or F)				
Sibling (M or F)				
Sibling (M or F)				
Sibling (M or F)				
Child (M or F)				
Child (M or F)				
Child (M or F)				
Child (M or F)				
Child (M or F)				

Conditions	Father	Mother	Sibling	Child	NOTES
Alcoholism					
Alzheimer's Disease					
Arthritis					
Asthma / Allergies					
Cancer					
Dementia					
Diabetes					
Epilepsy					
Gastritis / Ulcers					
Glaucoma					
Heart Disease / Issues					
Hepatitis					
High Cholesterol					
Hypertension / High Blood Pressure					
Kidney Diseases					
Lupus					
Migraine Headaches					
Osteoporosis					
Pancreatitis					
Polyneuropathy / Neurological Issues					
Stroke					
Thyroid Disorders					
OTHER:					

Vital Signs / Current Condition Chart

Date		Time	
Temperature		Pulse	
Blood Pressure		Respiratory Rate	
Urinary Continence		Bowel Control	
Stool Consistency		Mobility Status	
Food Intake		Hygiene Level	
Skin Color		Eye Clarity	
TOTAL POINTS			

Vital Signs / Current Condition Chart

Date		Time	
Temperature		Pulse	
Blood Pressure		Respiratory Rate	
Urinary Continence		Bowel Control	
Stool Consistency		Mobility Status	
Food Intake		Hygiene Level	
Skin Color		Eye Clarity	
TOTAL POINTS			

Vital Signs / Current Condition Chart

Date		Time	
Temperature		Pulse	
Blood Pressure		Respiratory Rate	
Urinary Continence		Bowel Control	
Stool Consistency		Mobility Status	
Food Intake		Hygiene Level	
Skin Color		Eye Clarity	
TOTAL POINTS			

Lab Results Tracking Chart

Test	Jan	Feb	Mar	Apr	May	Jun	Jul	Aug	Sep	Oct	Nov	Dec
INR												
Prothrombin Time												
Ammonia, Plasma												
Magnesium, Serum												
RBC												
Creatinine, Serum												
Potassium, Serum												

Lab Results Tracking Chart

Test	Jan	Feb	Mar	Apr	May	Jun	Jul	Aug	Sep	Oct	Nov	Dec
INR												
Prothrombin Time												
Ammonia, Plasma												
Magnesium, Serum												
RBC												
Creatinine, Serum												
Potassium, Serum												

Lab Results Tracking Chart

Test	Jan	Feb	Mar	Apr	May	Jun	Jul	Aug	Sep	Oct	Nov	Dec
INR												
Prothrombin Time												
Ammonia, Plasma												
Magnesium, Serum												
RBC												
Creatinine, Serum												
Potassium, Serum												

Test	Jan	Feb	Mar	Apr	May	Jun	July	Aug	Sept	Oct	Nov	Dec
Albumin, Serum												
Bilirubin, Total												
Alkaline Phosphatase												
AST												
ALT												

Liver Function Tracking Chart

Liver Function Tracking Chart

Test	Jan	Feb	Mar	Apr	May	Jun	July	Aug	Sept	Oct	Nov	Dec
Albumin, Serum												
Bilirubin, Total												
Alkaline Phosphatase												
AST												
ALT												

Liver Function Tracking Chart

Test	Jan	Feb	Mar	Apr	May	Jun	July	Aug	Sept	Oct	Nov	Dec
Albumin, Serum												
Bilirubin, Total												
Alkaline Phosphatase												
AST												
ALT												

Liver Function Tracking Chart

Test	Jan	Feb	Mar	Apr	May	Jun	July	Aug	Sept	Oct	Nov	Dec
Albumin, Serum												
Bilirubin, Total												
Alkaline Phosphatase												
AST												
ALT												

Child-Pugh Score Calculation Chart

Function	Points		
Total bilirubin			
Serum albumin			
Prothrombin time (INR)			
Ascities			
Hepatic Encephalopathy			
TOTAL POINTS			
CLASS			
One Year Survival Percentage		Two Year Survival Percentage	

Child-Pugh Score Calculation Chart

Function	Points		
Total bilirubin			
Serum albumin			
Prothrombin time (INR)			
Ascities			
Hepatic Encephalopathy			
TOTAL POINTS			
CLASS			
One Year Survival Percentage		Two Year Survival Percentage	

Child-Pugh Score Calculation Chart

Function	Points		
Total bilirubin			
Serum albumin			
Prothrombin time (INR)			
Ascities			
Hepatic Encephalopathy			
TOTAL POINTS			
CLASS			
One Year Survival Percentage		Two Year Survival Percentage	

Child Pugh Record Chart

Date	Points	Class	% Rate of Survival	
			One Year	Two Year

.

Detoxification History Record

Dates Entered		Dated Exited		Completed Detox?	
Entered By	Voluntary		Court Ordered		Intervention	
Mental State	Conscious			Unconscious	
Transported via	Private Vehicle		Ambulance		Other	
Name of Center					
Address					
Phone Number					
Notes					

Detoxification History Record

Dates Entered		Dated Exited		Completed Detox?	
Entered By	Voluntary		Court Ordered		Intervention	
Mental State	Conscious			Unconscious	
Transported via	Private Vehicle		Ambulance		Other	
Name of Center					
Address					
Phone Number					
Notes					

Rehabilitation History Records

Dates Entered		Dated Exited		Completed Program ?		
Entered By	Voluntary		Court Ordered		Intervention	
Resumed Drinking		How long after exiting did drinking resume				
Name of Center						
Address						
Phone Number						
Notes						

Rehabilitation History Records

Dates Entered		Dated Exited		Completed Program ?		
Entered By	Voluntary		Court Ordered		Intervention	
Resumed Drinking		How long after exiting did drinking resume				
Name of Center						
Address						
Phone Number						
Notes						

Rehabilitation History Records

Dates Entered		Dated Exited		Completed Program ?		
Entered By	Voluntary		Court Ordered		Intervention	
Resumed Drinking		How long after exiting did drinking resume				
Name of Center						
Address						
Phone Number						
Notes						

Summary of Condition Chart

Test	Jan	Feb	Mar	Apr	May	June	July	Aug	Sept	Oct	Nov	Dec
Overall Condition												
INR												
Prothrombin Time												
Ammonia, Plasma												
Magnesium, Serum												
RBC												
Creatinine, Serum												
Potassium, Serum												
Albumin, Serum												
Bilirubin, Total												
Alkaline Phosphatase												
AST (SGOT)												
ALT (SGPT)												
MELD												
Child-Pugh												

Overall Condition – Summary Graphs

	Jan	Feb	Mar	Apr	May	June	July	Aug	Sept	Oct	Nov	Dec
3												
4												
5												
6												
7												
8												
9												
10												
11												
12												
13												
14												
15												
16												
17												
18												
19												
20												
21												
22												
23												
24												

General Lab Results Charts

INR

	Jan	Feb	Mar	Apr	May	June	July	Aug	Sept	Oct	Nov	Dec
.08												
.09												
1.0												
1.1												
1.2												
1.4												
1.6												
1.8												
2.0												
2.2												
2.4												
2.6												
2.8												
2.9												
3.0												

Prothrombin Time

	Jan	Feb	Mar	Apr	May	June	July	Aug	Sept	Oct	Nov	Dec
11.2												
11.4												
11.6												
11.8												
12												
12.2												
12.4												
12.6												
12.8												
13												
13.2												
13.4												
13.6												
13.8												

Ammonia, Plasm

	Jan	Feb	Mar	Apr	May	June	July	Aug	Sept	Oct	Nov	Dec
102												
150												
200												
250												
300												
350												
400												
450												
500												
550												
600												
650												

RBC

	Jan	Feb	Mar	Apr	May	June	July	Aug	Sept	Oct	Nov	Dec
4.20												
4.10												
4												
3.80												
3.60												
3.40												
3.20												
3.10												
3												
2.80												
2.60												
2.40												
2.20												
2.10												
2												

Magnesium, Serum

	Jan	Feb	Mar	Apr	May	June	July	Aug	Sept	Oct	Nov	Dec
2.0												
1.6												
1.4												
1.2												
1												
.08												
.06												
.04												

Creatinine, Serum

	Jan	Feb	Mar	Apr	May	June	July	Aug	Sept	Oct	Nov	Dec
1.2												
.08												
.76												
.74												
.72												
.70												
.68												
.64												
.62												
.6												
.58												
.56												
.54												

Potassium, Serum

	Jan		Feb		Mar		Apr		May		June		July		Aug		Sept		Oct		Nov		Dec	
4																								
3.5																								
3.4																								
3.2																								
3																								
2.8																								
2.6																								
2.4																								
2.2																								
2																								
1.8																								
1.6																								

Liver Function Tests Charts

Albumin, Serum

	Jan	Feb	Mar	Apr	May	June	July	Aug	Sept	Oct	Nov	Dec
4.0												
3.8												
3.6												
3.4												
3.2												
3												
2.8												
2.6												
2.4												
2.2												
2												
1.8												
1.6												
1.4												

Bilirubin, Total

	Jan	Feb	Mar	Apr	May	June	July	Aug	Sept	Oct	Nov	Dec
2.8												
3												
3.5												
4												
4.5												
5												
5.5												
6												
6.5												
7												
7.5												
8												
8.5												
9												
9.5												
10												

Alkaline Phosphatase

	Jan	Feb	Mar	Apr	May	June	July	Aug	Sept	Oct	Nov	Dec
180												
200												
250												
300												
350												
400												
450												
500												

AST (SGOT)

	Jan	Feb	Mar	Apr	May	June	July	Aug	Sept	Oct	Nov	Dec
50												
100												
150												
200												
250												
300												
350												
400												
450												
500												

ALT (SGPT)

	Jan	Feb	Mar	Apr	May	June	July	Aug	Sept	Oct	Nov	Dec
50												
55												
70												
80												
100												
150												
200												
250												
300												
350												
400												
450												
500												

MELD and Child-Pugh Scores Charts

MELD

	Jan	Feb	Mar	Apr	May	June	July	Aug	Sept	Oct	Nov	Dec
40												
35												
30												
28												
26												
24												
22												
20												
18												
16												
14												
12												
10												
8												
6												

Child-Pugh Score (based on total points)

	Jan	Feb	Mar	Apr	May	June	July	Aug	Sept	Oct	Nov	Dec
6												
7												
9												
10												
11												
12												
13												
14												
16												

CPSIA information can be obtained
at www.ICGtesting.com
Printed in the USA
LVHW100812110219
607093LV00012BA/199/P